DISCARD

COMPACT *Research*

Teenage Dropouts

Teenage Problems

ReferencePoint
Press®

San Diego, CA

Other books in the Compact Research Teenage Problems set:

Teenage Alcoholism
Teenage Drug Abuse
Teenage Eating Disorders
Teenage Mental Illness
Teenage Sex and Pregnancy
Teenage Suicide
Teen Violence

COMPACT *Research*

Teenage Dropouts

Gail B. Stewart

Teenage Problems

ReferencePoint
Press®

San Diego, CA

© 2013 ReferencePoint Press, Inc.
Printed in the United States

For more information, contact:
ReferencePoint Press, Inc.
PO Box 27779
San Diego, CA 92198
www.ReferencePointPress.com

LIBRARY OF CONGRESS CATALOGING-IN-PUBLICATION DATA

Stewart, Gail B. (Gail Barbara), 1949–
  Teenage dropouts / by Gail B. Stewart.
    pages cm. -- (Compact research series)
  Includes bibliographical references and index.
  ISBN-13: 978-1-60152-506-2 (hardback)
  ISBN-10: 1-60152-506-0 (hardback)
1. High school dropouts--United States--Juvenile literature. 2. Dropouts--United States--Juvenile literature. 3. Educational sociology. I. Title.
  LC146.6.S75   2013
  373.12'9130973--dc23
                                                                    2012036648

Contents

Foreword

"Where is the knowledge we have lost in information?"

—T.S. Eliot, "The Rock."

As modern civilization continues to evolve, its ability to create, store, distribute, and access information expands exponentially. The explosion of information from all media continues to increase at a phenomenal rate. By 2020 some experts predict the worldwide information base will double every seventy-three days. While access to diverse sources of information and perspectives is paramount to any democratic society, information alone cannot help people gain knowledge and understanding. Information must be organized and presented clearly and succinctly in order to be understood. The challenge in the digital age becomes not the creation of information, but how best to sort, organize, enhance, and present information.

ReferencePoint Press developed the *Compact Research* series with this challenge of the information age in mind. More than any other subject area today, researching current issues can yield vast, diverse, and unqualified information that can be intimidating and overwhelming for even the most advanced and motivated researcher. The *Compact Research* series offers a compact, relevant, intelligent, and conveniently organized collection of information covering a variety of current topics ranging from illegal immigration and deforestation to diseases such as anorexia and meningitis.

The series focuses on three types of information: objective single-author narratives, opinion-based primary source quotations, and facts and statistics. The clearly written objective narratives provide context and reliable background information. Primary source quotes are carefully selected and cited, exposing the reader to differing points of view, and facts and statistics sections aid the reader in evaluating perspectives. Presenting these key types of information creates a richer, more balanced learning experience.

For better understanding and convenience, the series enhances information by organizing it into narrower topics and adding design features that make it easy for a reader to identify desired content. For example, in *Compact Research: Illegal Immigration*, a chapter covering the economic impact of illegal immigration has an objective narrative explaining the various ways the economy is impacted, a balanced section of numerous primary source quotes on the topic, followed by facts and full-color illustrations to encourage evaluation of contrasting perspectives.

The ancient Roman philosopher Lucius Annaeus Seneca wrote, "It is quality rather than quantity that matters." More than just a collection of content, the *Compact Research* series is simply committed to creating, finding, organizing, and presenting the most relevant and appropriate amount of information on a current topic in a user-friendly style that invites, intrigues, and fosters understanding.

Teenage Dropouts at a Glance

Prevalence

More than 1.2 million teens each year make the decision to drop out of high school before graduating.

Minority Students

The dropout rate for minority students in 2012 was as high as 45 to 50 percent, according to *THE Journal*.

Reasons for Dropping Out

Dropouts give a number of reasons for their decision—among them, pregnancy, difficulty with schoolwork, too many absences, suspensions, and the need to work to help their family.

Job Problems for Dropouts

Dropouts often lack the skill necessary for many twenty-first-century jobs. According to College and Career Connection in Washington, DC, high school dropouts are ineligible for 90 percent of all jobs in today's economy.

Lower Wages over a Lifetime

According to a 2011 report by the National Center for Education Statistics, a dropout will earn about $660,000 less over a lifetime than someone who has earned at least a GED.

Crime

Statistics show that dropouts are far more likely to be incarcerated than high school graduates.

The Cost to US Taxpayers

Dropouts cost taxpayers hundreds of billions of dollars each year in lost wages, taxable income, welfare, and incarceration costs.

Preventing Teens from Dropping Out

Some experts believe states might prevent more dropouts by raising the age requirement for students to stay in high school; others feel schools need to be more flexible in their curricula and teaching styles.

Helping Dropouts

Often dropouts can benefit from programs that pair discipline and learning new skills with academic work toward a GED or high school diploma.

Overview

❝It is gut-wrenching that 1.2 million students in U.S. public schools fail to earn their high school diploma each year.❞

—Nakia Hill, multimedia journalist and GED preparation teacher.

❝The transition to adulthood is likely to be perilous and rocky for young people who drop out of high school.❞

—Dan Bloom, evaluator of programs and policies designed for high school dropouts at MDRC, a nonprofit education research organization.

L iving with his girlfriend in a suburb north of Saint Paul, Minnesota, eighteen-year-old Glenn spends most of his days working on his car or playing video games. He dropped out of school after tenth grade. He had a job for eight weeks at a discount store, but then it ended. And though he has applied for several jobs since then, Glenn has not yet been called for an interview. Despite still being unemployed, he says he has not changed his mind about finishing school. "I was never a good student," he says. "I don't think I'm a slow learner or anything—I just don't like studying or reading. I'd rather be doing something outside or being with my friends. I guess I haven't found the subjects they teach very interesting. History, no. English, no. Science, no. Math, no. I'm just a lot happier not being there anymore."[1]

Does the United States Have a Dropout Problem?

Every school day in the United States, seven thousand students make the decision to drop out before graduating. That translates to one new dropout every twenty-six seconds. In 2011 more than 1.2 million students throughout the United States withdrew from high school without earning a diploma.

The effects of dropping out are most apparent in terms of income-earning ability. According to a 2011 study by the US Department of Education, high school dropouts can expect to earn far less over their lifetime than their more-educated peers. The study found that a high school dropout would earn only about 40 cents for every dollar earned by a college graduate.

Society suffers, too, when teens drop out of school. Because so many dropouts are unemployed or underemployed, they pay far fewer taxes and thus provide less revenue for the communities and states in which they live. A study released in 2011 by the Center for Labor Market Studies at Northeastern University found that 32 percent of dropouts depend on food stamps, compared with 17.3 percent of high school graduates. Too, male dropouts are far more likely than male high school graduates to be incarcerated—14.7 percent, as opposed to only 3 percent of male high school graduates.

> " The effects of dropping out are most apparent in terms of income-earning ability. "

The History of the Dropout Problem

The concept of a "dropout" is a relatively new one in US history. In 1900 only about 6 percent of young adults graduated from high school. Most children in those days stopped going to school after elementary school. Only if a student was interested in a career that required more than a basic elementary school education, such as being a doctor or a lawyer, for example, was high school (and then college) an option worth pursuing. The average person could function just fine with only a basic education in reading, writing, and math.

Only in the years following World War II have a majority of US teenagers graduated from high school. This change came about for several reasons. One had to do with an increase in the number of immigrants coming to the United States; many of these immigrants tended to compete with teenagers for low-skill jobs. Another reason for the rise in American teens completing high school was enforcement of tougher child labor laws, such as the Fair Labor Standards Act of 1938, which made it illegal to hire children under sixteen for full-time work. As a result, more teens stayed in high school, and about 50 percent graduated.

Many of those who left early had jobs or apprenticeships lined up. They were often referred to as "withdrawers" or "early leavers"—terms that were considered neither critical nor negative.

> " In the twenty-first century, the dropout rate is not balanced equally among ethnic and racial groups. "

The term *dropout* came into use in the early 1960s, at a time when a four-year high school education had become the norm. By then, because so many teens were graduating, those who left early began to be viewed as failures or even troublemakers. In 1963 President John F. Kennedy introduced a nationwide Summer Dropout Campaign to call attention to the growing number of teens leaving school early. He was the first president to characterize dropping out of school as a sign of failure—as much for society as for the individual: "Ignorance and illiteracy, unskilled workers and school dropouts—these and other failures of our educational system breed failures in our social and economic system: delinquency, unemployment, chronic dependence, a waste of human resources, a loss of productive power and an increase in tax-supported benefits."[2]

Continued Concern

Efforts to increase the high school graduation rate continued, with the introduction of a variety of anti-dropout initiatives. In 1990 President George H.W. Bush pushed to increase the national graduation rate to 90 percent, and in 2001 Congress passed President George W. Bush's No Child Left Behind Act. The intent of the law was to improve public education by holding schools responsible and accountable for increasing their graduation rates. Many criticized No Child Left Behind for the rigid timetable given schools to show improved achievement by students, as well as the emphasis on frequent testing. Some critics said that the law encouraged teachers to let struggling students drop out so they would not lower the school's test scores.

More than 1.2 million US students dropped out of high school in 2011. The highest dropout rates occur among Hispanic, African American, and Native American youth.

Recently, America's Promise Alliance, led by General Colin Powell and his wife, Alma, refocused efforts in 2010 to move the high school graduation rate to 90 percent, but with less emphasis on constant testing. President Barack Obama supported the new effort, warning, "The stakes are too high—for our children, for our economy, and for our country. It's time for all of us to come together—parents, students, principals and teachers, business leaders and elected officials from across the political spectrum—to end America's dropout crisis."[3]

Race and Ethnicity

In the twenty-first century, the dropout rate is not balanced equally among ethnic and racial groups. One of the most troubling aspects of the dropout problem is that its effects are felt the most in groups that are already struggling financially in the United States—Hispanics, African Americans, and Native Americans.

Statistics released in 2011 by the Department of Education show that the graduation rate for American high school students as a whole is 75 percent. However, a Hispanic or African American student has less than a 65 percent chance of graduating. Native Americans and Native Alaskans fare worst, graduating at about 55 percent. Comparatively, the graduation rates of white and Asian students is 82 and 84 percent, respectively.

> **Each of the fifty states had at least one school designated as a dropout factory.**

Critics complain that in some schools, teachers and administrators see high rates of failure and dropping out among teens of color as normal and, in too many cases, both predictable and acceptable. In his PBS special, *Too Important to Fail*, correspondent Tavis Smiley interviews author and educational expert Jawanza Kunjufu about the low expectations schools have for black children—especially boys. Kunjufu contends that the response among school administrators and teachers is far different than it would be if the educational results among white children and black children were reversed:

> If 53 percent was the dropout [rate] for white males, it would be unacceptable; if 41 percent of their children were being placed in special education, that would be a major crisis. If only 20 percent of their boys were proficient in reading in eighth grade, that would be a crisis. If only 2.5 of white males ever earned a college degree, that would be a major crisis in America.[4]

Why Do Students Drop Out?

Guidance counselors and other experts say that there are many reasons that students make the decision to drop out of school. Some are like Glenn—teens who are uninterested in academics and tend to do poorly on tests and projects. Many frequently skip school, and their absences make success even more difficult. Others leave because they feel bullied or otherwise victimized by classmates.

Some experts cite the need to work as a reason many teens are dropping out of school—usually with the approval of their families. Since the US economic recession began in 2007, teachers and administrators have seen an increase in parents who feel that the family is better served with their teenagers working. "The economy is affecting everyone, including students," said Christine Luzi, who leads the guidance department at Framingham High School in Massachusetts. "More of them are having to work to support their families. They're helping their parents pay the phone bill or the electricity bill."[5]

Some guidance counselors say that balancing schoolwork with a job can present serious difficulties for some students. More and more fall behind in their class work, and some end up dropping out of school. One Milwaukee-area high school counselor worries that too many teens who start out working part-time to help their families may become less involved in even the social aspects of school. That, she says, can make it easier to increase their work hours and drop out altogether:

> Maybe they don't try out for a team because they work those after-school hours. Or maybe they just don't have the money to spend on going to a dance, or the time to attend Homecoming activities or whatever. I've seen students that are so focused on their after-school job, they just lose interest in keeping up with classes that they used to enjoy. They gradually sort of pull away from their school life—academic as well as social. That's a loss—for them as much as for the school.[6]

Pregnant Dropouts

For girls, pregnancy is a common reason for dropping out of high school. According to America's Promise Alliance, approximately 30 percent of girls who leave school do so because they are pregnant or because they have recently given birth. The rates for African American and Hispanic girls are higher—38 percent and 36 percent respectively, as reported by the National Center for Education Statistics in 2011.

Educators say they are frustrated by teenage pregnancy rates because of the way these rates influence decisions to leave school early. Although the rate of teenage pregnancy has declined to its lowest level since its peak in 1990, teenaged girls in the United States continue to have the

Pregnancy is a common reason for teen girls to drop out of high school. Less than half of the girls who quit school because of pregnancy ever return to get their diplomas.

highest rate of pregnancies in the developed world—750,000 annually. That is nine times higher than most developed nations. According to the National Campaign to Prevent Teen and Unplanned Pregnancy, only 38 percent of teens under age eighteen who drop out because of pregnancy ever return to school for a high school diploma.

Dropout Factories

Experts have found that it is the schools themselves that sometimes contribute to the dropout problem. Some of the lowest-performing schools in the country—that is, those with the highest dropout rates—have been described as dropout factories. In 2002 Johns Hopkins University researchers categorized a school as a dropout factory if it graduated 60 percent or fewer of its students. In such a school, by the time a freshman class reaches its senior year, it has shrunk by 40 percent or more.

The nearly two thousand dropout factories originally identified in 2002—about 13 percent of American high schools—ranged from large inner-city or suburban high schools to small rural schools. They produced half of the nation's dropouts, and 75 percent of the African American and Hispanic teens that dropped out. Each of the fifty states had at least one school designated as a dropout factory, according to the Alliance for Excellent Education.

In recent years efforts to fix or do away with such schools have had some success. As of 2012 the number of dropout factories had shrunk by more than 450 since 2002, but experts were dissatisfied that 1,550 were still operating. "The reality," says US secretary of education Arne Duncan, "is that even one dropout factory is too many."[7]

Experiencing a Dropout Factory

Nelson Reidar, a forty-one-year veteran teacher and principal, spent a year in a California school that was classified as a dropout factory. Discouraged and upset by what he saw on a day-to-day basis, Reidar wrote a book about his experiences, *Education Malpractice: A Year in a Dropout Factory*. The term *dropout factory* definitely applies to Reidar's Southern California school, which he does not name, at the request of his publisher. Instead, he refers to the school as Red Bird City. Red Bird City's class of 2011 started out in 2007 with 1,280 ninth graders. By 2011 the class had dwindled to 495 students. Only 378 students, or 30 percent of the original class, graduated at the end of the 2011 school year.

In his book Reidar criticizes the frequency with which teachers handed out suspensions, rather than working with the students who caused problems. During the year that he was there, Red Bird City had a suspension rate of 108 percent, meaning that about twenty-five hundred suspension days were handed down to twenty-three hundred students. Because California allocates money for schools based on attendance, all of those suspensions cost the school $110,000 in funding.

Even more disturbing, Reidar commented, was the indifference exhibited by members of school faculty and staff. For example, he describes a male teacher who regularly gave his students mundane textbook assignments to do while he surfed the web during class time. "It's just crazy," Reidar says, "to think that he thinks he's doing a good job."[8]

How Can the United States Reduce the Dropout Rate?

Education experts say that there are many strategies that have already shown success in keeping students in school. One is the importance of recognizing signs that a student may be on the path to dropping out—even before he or she realizes it. Among these signs are frequent absences, difficulty with core classes such as math or reading, and chronic misbehavior in school.

Education expert Robert Balfanz of Johns Hopkins University has done studies indicating that if even one such sign is visible in middle school, there is a 75 percent chance that that student will drop out in the future. By recognizing those signs, teachers can take action such as urging the student to repeat a grade or providing intensive help so the student can get back on track academically.

> " Schools can also be a strong force for solving the problems that threaten a student's ability to remain in school. "

However, the newest research shows that some of these signs of impending school failure may be evident even earlier—as soon as third grade. In 2012 the City University of New York released the findings of a study that analyzed the reading scores and graduation rates of almost four thousand students born between 1979 and 1989. The study found that one in six of them who could not read at grade level back in third grade had not finished high school by age nineteen.

The dropout rate of that group was four times the rate of proficient readers. Many experts believe such data suggest that it would be better to hold such students back while they are very young than allow them to get further and further behind as they progress through school. However, some educators cite studies that find students who are held back in school suffer a range of negative effects, including bullying by classmates and a loss of confidence and self-esteem. Others worry that retaining children may be too expensive. Currently, the United States spends $12 million a year on students who repeat a grade.

> " A growing number of community and technical colleges are offering dropouts a way to enter college without a high school diploma. "

The Use of Vital Data

Schools can also be a strong force for solving the problems that threaten a student's ability to remain in school. Dropout prevention can be as simple as alert teachers or staff noticing something amiss with a student and doing something about it. In New York City the staff at Middle School 244 in the Bronx has shown that being aware of the predictors of future dropouts can be crucial. Middle School 244's principal, Dolores Peterson, holds regular meetings with teachers and staff to address situations that could develop into dropout problems. One such situation involved a talented student named Omarina, whose tardiness and absences had become increasingly frequent.

In consulting her teachers and counselor, the principal learned that Omarina and her mother had been evicted from a shelter weeks before, and the middle schooler was now being shuttled among relatives. The expense and confusion of ever-changing routes of buses and trains made getting to school difficult for her. Embarrassed by the chaos in her family, Omarina had not confided in her teachers. But her attendance and tardiness records were strong indicators of a problem, and once the school staff understood the problem, they helped solve it.

The staff purchased a bus pass for Omarina, and her teachers helped her work out the easiest routes to take from various relatives' homes so she could arrive on time for school. As Catherine Miller, Omarina's homeroom teacher, explains, data alone is meaningless. "We can compile thousands of numbers about who's failing this and who's passing that," she says, "but if there's no response to that data, if there's no initiative taken to understand that data, it's all for naught."[9]

Can Dropouts Be Helped?

Education experts can point to a number of ways they are helping young people who have already dropped out of school. Some are alternative schools that offer flexible hours, intensive individual reading and math help for those who need it, and even on-site child care. Many of these alternative programs are either free or offered at very low cost to students.

Some of the most successful ways of helping dropouts involve programs that merge high school classes with college classes. One such program, developed with grant money from the Bill & Melinda Gates Foundation, is known as Gateway to College. A growing number of community and technical colleges are offering dropouts a way to enter college without a high school diploma. The Gateway to College program was started in 2003 with the idea of giving sixteen- to twenty-year-old at-risk youth the opportunity to earn a high school diploma and college credits at the same place.

"They are coming into a college setting and a more adult atmosphere and being exposed to college instructors," says Tarmara Williams, associate vice provost of academic services at Owens Community College near Toledo, Ohio. "They will have resource specialists, coaches, and mentors to help them complete a high school diploma and obtain college credit." She adds, "It's really a way to re-engage students and give them a second opportunity."[10]

High school dropouts face many challenges, but programs are in place to help at-risk students stay in school or go back to school once they have quit. Those who persevere are more likely to achieve their goals—which is a positive outcome for the students and for society.

Does the United States Have a Dropout Problem?

"In 1970, the United States had the world's highest rate of high school and college graduation. Today, according to the Organization for Economic Cooperation and Development, we've slipped to No. 21 in high school completion and No. 15 in college completion."

—Henry M. Levin, a professor of economics and education at Teachers College at Columbia University, and Cecilia E. Rouse, a professor of economics and public affairs at Princeton University.

"I can't tell you how many guys I know who've already left school. They could care less about graduating. I had a friend in Chicago who dropped out before he turned 15."

—Gabe, a Wisconsin dropout who left school at age seventeen.

Marco Williams did not plan on dropping out of high school midway through eleventh grade. His goal was to graduate and then become an auto mechanic. Always good with car engines, he knew he could be good enough to open his own shop someday. But his plans were derailed when his girlfriend became pregnant. Williams reluctantly left school to find a job and support his new family.

At first he was confident that he could find work at a repair shop, or maybe even a local auto dealership, but he soon learned that was not possible. He says:

> They won't even look at you without a diploma, and even then, you've got to take more classes after that. You've got to get certified, and you can't do that without a high school diploma. I had no chance of doing any of that, at least right then. So my only prospects were busing tables at a restaurant part-time, and working the overnight shift at the gas station—both minimum wage jobs, with zero benefits. And I'm working both jobs. I love my girlfriend and my baby, but this is really not what I planned for my life, you know?[11]

Problems with Statistics

Williams is one of the approximately 1.2 million American teens who drop out of school each year. According to the Alliance for Excellent Education, a Washington, DC–based education advocacy organization, nearly one out of every four ninth graders entering high school will drop out by their senior year.

As startling as those statistics are, many experts believe that the numbers may actually be much higher. The problem with determining a correct number is that schools have different ways of defining the term *dropout*. Some do not consider students to be dropouts if they leave school and later enroll in adult education or a General Equivalency Degree (GED) program. Some schools do not consider a student a dropout if he or she commits a crime and is sent to juvenile detention or, if over eighteen years old, to prison before completing school. Many schools count students as dropouts only if they officially withdraw from a school.

> " The financial threat posed by a high dropout rate is considerable. "

A 2011 report by National Public Radio found that underreporting dropout rates often occurs because admitting a dropout problem can be detrimental to a school. Explains National Public Radio reporter Claudio

Sanchez, "It is not in the interest of schools to have an honest, accurate account of dropouts—not just because a high dropout rate makes a school look bad, but also because there's serious money at stake. Most schools get funded based on attendance. If kids don't show up, schools lose money."[12]

The financial threat posed by a high dropout rate is considerable. In 2009, for example, the Chicago school district lost an estimated $18 million to $20 million in state funding because of its attendance statis-

> **High school dropouts are ineligible for 90 percent of the jobs in today's economy.**

tics. Some schools have been accused of fabricating attendance records, counting students on their rolls who have long since dropped out, to avoid such hits to their state funding. "When you have that kind of pressure, human beings tend to cheat,"[13] notes William Gerstein, principal of Chicago's Austin Polytechnical Academy High School.

Finding a Job

The number one problem faced by dropouts is their inability to get a job. Because they have not finished school, dropouts make up the least-educated part of the workforce. As a result, they often lack the skills and technical knowledge that are necessary for jobs in the twenty-first century. According to College & Career Connection, an organization dedicated to inspiring students from low-income communities in Washington, DC, to graduate from high school and pursue higher education, high school dropouts are ineligible for 90 percent of the jobs in today's economy.

The job market of the twenty-first century is much different than the job market a few decades ago. In the 1950s and 1960s, it was still possible for someone to get a well-paying job without a high school diploma. Harry Welch, age seventy, dropped out of high school when he turned seventeen. He knew he wanted to be a carpenter, working with his father in the cabinetry business. "I raised a family on my salary," says Welch. "I didn't need a diploma for that. My wife and I weren't rich, but we bought a house, had four great kids, a nice life. I'd never be able to do that these days."[14]

Today's dropouts are far less likely to find jobs, and those who do secure a job usually receive the lowest wages, earning just forty cents to every dollar earned by a college graduate. The difference in wages between high school dropouts and high school graduates who have not completed college is also considerable. A 2011 report by the National Center for Education Statistics estimates that a dropout will earn approximately $630,000 less over his or her lifetime than someone who has earned at least a GED.

Dropouts in the Recession

The economic recession that began in December 2007 has created hardships for many Americans. With less money to spend, consumers have been forced to minimize their purchases. Faced with fewer customers for their products or services, some businesses have closed, while others have scaled back the number of workers on their payroll.

Experts say that it is an unfortunate fact of life that when hard times hit, those in the lowest-paying jobs are the first to be laid off. Statistics for the recession bear that out. During the recession, the national unemployment rate jumped from 5 percent in 2007 to 8.2 percent as of July 2012. However, the unemployment rate for dropouts during this time was far higher, ranging from 15 percent to 18 percent, according to a 2012 report by National Public Radio.

Predictably, anytime a job did become available, companies were flooded with applicants. The National Public Radio study found that to narrow the pool, many employers began requiring that an applicant have a high school diploma—even for less-skilled jobs. Raymond Smith, the owner of a small commercial cleaning business in suburban Chicago, recently had ninety calls in a single morning about a job opening. He says one of the first questions he asked of the applicants was whether they graduated from high school. Smith says:

> That tells me something about the person who wants the job. Does having a high school diploma mean he or she can clean an office better? No, of course not. But I look at it like this: a diploma means that individual stuck with school, showed up most of the time, and finished, even though maybe school was hard. I think the one with the diploma is a lot more likely to be a reliable employee.[15]

Health and Well-Being

Being unemployed—or, if working, trapped in a low-end job—presents a wide range of hardships. Dropouts are far more likely to rely on welfare to get by—from food stamps to government assistance for housing. In 2011, 32 percent of dropouts received food stamps, compared to 17 percent of high school graduates.

Health is another issue for dropouts. The National Center for Health Statistics conducts health interview surveys in which they ask people to rate their own health. In 2009, the most recent year for which data are available, 52.2 percent of high school graduates rated themselves as being in excellent or very good health. However, only 38 percent of dropouts felt the same way. Such statistics beg the question: Does having a high school diploma make a person healthier?

In fact, public health officials have known for years that level of education is one of the strongest means of predicting health. They have found that death rates among people of a similar age are lower among those who are better educated. The life expectancy for a dropout is nine years less than that of a high school graduate. The diseases most likely to contribute to 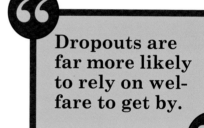 this are lung cancer, heart disease, and stroke. Dropouts also suffer more from anxiety and depression than those with more education.

> Dropouts are far more likely to rely on welfare to get by.

The reasons for the difference in health vary. One is that dropouts are less likely to have a job with health-care benefits. As a result, they and their family members are less able to afford routine checkups that can spot a health problem before it becomes serious. They are less likely to have the money or opportunity to join a gym, attend an aerobics class, or participate in a softball league—all good ways to stay fit. Health experts also find that the less education people have, the more likely they are to smoke, use illegal drugs, become overweight, or avoid exercise—all indicators of future poor health.

Crime

Dropouts face other challenges, too. Dropouts are far more likely than high school graduates to commit crimes and be incarcerated either in federal or state prison. A 2009 study conducted by Northeastern University found that on any given day, about one in every ten young male high school dropouts is either in jail or in juvenile detention. The statistics for young African American males—one in four—are even more disturbing. "We're trying to show what it means to be a dropout in the 21st century United States," explained Andrew Sum, the director of the study. "It's one of the country's costliest problems. The unemployment, the incarceration rates—it's scary."[16]

> In fact, society as a whole suffers the consequences when teens drop out.

Besides being more at risk for criminal behavior, dropouts tend to be nonparticipants in their communities, even in adulthood. They tend not to volunteer in churches or community organizations, work with young people, or even donate blood. They also are less likely to vote. For example, in the 2008 presidential election, whereas 52 percent of high school graduates voted, only 37 percent of dropouts cast ballots, according to statistics from the US Department of Commerce.

A Heavy Burden for Society

But dropouts are not the only ones who suffer from their decision to leave school without a diploma. In fact, society as a whole suffers the consequences when teens drop out. With millions of dropouts not living up to their potential, there is a drain on the economy of the nation as well as individual states. According to Chicago's Aparecio Foundation, which works to empower young women to stay in school, dropouts annually cost taxpayers more than $8 billion in public assistance programs. According to the Center for Labor Market Studies, the costs to society amount to $250,000 for every teen who does not graduate from high school.

The loss of millions of dollars in revenue from potential workers also means that there is less money coming into the state and federal governments in the form of taxes. That translates into fewer dollars for public projects desperately needed by local and federal government. According to the Alliance of Excellent Education, simply cutting the dropout rate in half for one high school class in the fifty largest American cities would have dramatic results. Reducing that many dropouts would result in an annual $4.1 billion boost in earnings, which would create thirty thousand additional jobs and provide an extra $5.3 billion in economic growth.

Dropout Will Suffer

The more educated, skilled workers the United States produces, the stronger the nation's economy will be. With a better-educated workforce, the United States will be able to better compete in what has become a global economy. According to the Georgetown University Center on Education and the Workforce, by 2018 the United States will need 22 million new college graduates with degrees. However, because of the high dropout rate in high schools, there will be a shortage of college students to fill the need.

Experts believe that the nation will be about 3 million short of that 22 million. That means millions of jobs that should be done in the United States will go to skilled workers overseas. In a 2010 speech, Barack Obama expressed concern about the numbers of young people dropping out of school. He explained that America cannot compete in the global economy without a highly educated workforce:

> And we know that the success of every American will be tied more closely than ever before to the level of education they achieve. The jobs will go to the people with the knowledge and the skills to do them—it's that simple. In this kind of knowledge economy, giving up on your education and dropping out of school means not only giving up on your future, but it's also giving up on your family's future and your country's future.[17]

Primary Source Quotes*

Does the United States Have a Dropout Problem?

66 We need to oust the malingers, miscreants, goof-offs, and gang-bangers who are nothing but seat warmers, at best, and, at worst, a distraction or a danger to teachers and the majority of students who wish to carry out the school system's mission of obtaining a reasonable level of education for those who wish to become contributing members of a civil society. 99

—Thomas Mitchell, "The Real Problem with Nevada's Dropout Rate," February 20, 2011. www.lvrj.com.

Mitchell is senior opinion editor of the *Las Vegas (NV) Review-Journal*.

66 In addition to the moral imperative to provide every student with an equal opportunity to pursue the American dream, our nation's economic security now requires many more students to graduate from high school. 99

—Barack Obama, "Remarks by the President at the America's Promise Alliance Education Event," March 1, 2010. www.whitehouse.gov.

Barack Obama is the forty-fourth president of the United States.

* Editor's Note: While the definition of a primary source can be narrowly or broadly defined, for the purposes of Compact Research, a primary source consists of: 1) results of original research presented by an organization or researcher; 2) eyewitness accounts of events, personal experience, or work experience; 3) first-person editorials offering pundits' opinions; 4) government officials presenting political plans and/or policies; 5) representatives of organizations presenting testimony or policy.

Primary Source Quotes

66 **High school students who drop out and end up working in low-paying jobs will soon figure out the need for a decent education in order to improve their economic situation.** 99

—Phil Quon, "What Is the Solution to the High School Dropout Crisis?," *Education Experts Blog, National Journal*, September 21, 2009. http://education.nationaljournal.com.

Quon is the superintendent of the Cupertino Union School District in California.

66 **Unlike previous generations, for whom unskilled jobs were plentiful, young people who drop out today will be unable to find sustainable employment without gaining additional skills.** 99

—Kathleen A. Barfield, Jenifer Hartman, and Dixie Knight, "Early Warning Systems: It's Never Too Early," *THE Journal*, February–March 2012.

Barfield is chief information officer at Edvance Research, and Hartman is director of practice-based research and Knight development manager at the same facility.

66 **This isn't just about data or numbers. But these are real kids who, frankly, are pretty much consigned to dead-end jobs, public assistance or prison after dropping out of high school.** 99

—Robert Balfanz, "How Early Warning Systems Are Keeping Kids in School," *The Answer Sheet* (blog), *Washington Post*, April 10, 2012. www.washingtonpost.com.

Robert Balfanz is a senior research scientist at the Center for Social Organization of Schools at Johns Hopkins University.

66 **On all the indicators of academic achievement, educational attainment, and school success, African-American and Latino males are noticeably distinguished from other segments of the American population by their consistent clustering at the bottom.** 99

—Pedro A. Noguera, "Saving Black and Latino Boys: What Schools Can Do to Make a Difference," *Phi Beta Kappan*, February 2012.

Noguera is Peter L. Agnew Professor of Education at New York University.

"High school dropouts are bearing the brunt of the on-going recession more than the rest of the population."

—American Psychological Association, "Facing the Dropout Dilemma," April 20, 2012. www.apa.org.

The American Psychological Association is a scientific and professional organization that represents psychologists throughout the United States.

....

"Not only is the graduation rate in the United States generally low and highly variable, but it also appears to be getting worse."

—Russell W. Rumberger, *Dropping Out: Why Students Drop Out of High School and What Can Be Done About It.*
Cambridge, MA: Harvard University Press, 2011.

Rumberger is a professor of education at the University of California–Santa Barbara.

....

Facts and Illustrations

Does the United States Have a Dropout Problem?

- Only **7 percent** of dropouts aged twenty-five and older have ever made more than forty thousand dollars a year, National Public Radio reported in 2011.

- **Seven thousand** students drop out of school in the United States every day, according to the Alliance for Excellent Education.

- A 2009 Harvard University study found that **37 percent** of African American male high school dropouts were incarcerated.

- Students from **low-income** families are six times more likely to drop out than those from **higher-income** families, according to My Turn, a youth workforce development group.

- The lowest dropout rate among US ethnic groups is that of Asians/Pacific Islanders, at only **10 percent**.

- A 2012 study at the University of California–Santa Barbara estimates that over their lifetimes, just one year's worth of California high school dropouts will cost society **$24.2 billion** in lost revenue and welfare programs over the course of their lifetimes.

- The population of dropouts between the ages of sixteen and twenty-four in the United States in 2010 was estimated to be between **3.5 million and 6 million**, according to The Future of Children, a collaborative effort of Princeton University and the Brookings Institution.

Dropouts Fare Poorly in the Workplace

Data presented in a 2012 report called "Building a Grad Nation," showed that there are very strong differences between high school dropouts and those with high school or college diplomas in terms of both employment and income. In fact, a high school dropout's weekly income is approximately 25 percent of that of a college graduate.

Individual Economic Outcomes, by Education

Unemployment Rate in 2010

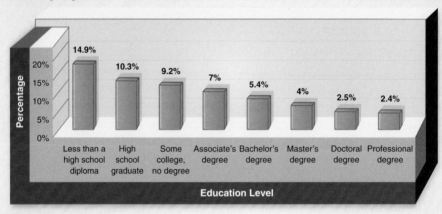

Median Weekly Earnings in 2010

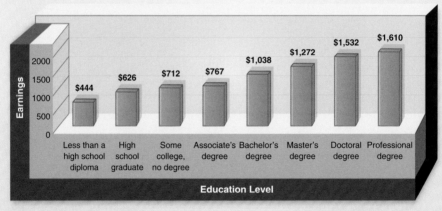

Source: Civic Enterprises, Everyone Graduates Center, America's Promise Alliance, and the Alliance for Excellent Education, "Building a Grad Nation: Progress and Challenge in Ending the High School Dropout Epidemic," 2012. www.civicenterprises.net.

School District Dropout Numbers, 2011

Experts know that the dropout problem is in city, suburban, and rural school districts. In a 2011 report by the American Public Health Association's Center for School, Health and Education, experts list the twenty-five US school districts which projected the most dropouts for 2011.

Dropout Epicenters, 2011			
Projected Dropouts	District	Projected Dropouts	District
39,669	New York City, NY	5,396	Orange County, FL
35,568	Los Angeles, CA	5,366	Gwinnett County, GA
16,114	Clark County, NV	5,044	San Diego, CA
11,310	Miami-Dade County, FL	5,000	Palm Beach County, FL
10,469	Chicago, IL	4,880	DeKalb County, GA
9,304	Philadelphia, PA	4,787	Charlotte-Mecklenburg, NC
8,039	Detroit, MI	4,315	Milwaukee, WI
7,852	Houston, TX	4,313	Kern Union, CA
7,477	Broward County, FL	4,260	Prince George's County, MD
6,990	Dallas, TX	4,209	Phoenix Union, CA
5,867	Hillsborough County, FL	4,109	Memphis, TN
5,550	Duval County, FL	3,963	Albuquerque, NM
5,523	Hawaii		

Source: American Public Health Association, Center for School, Health and Education, "The Dropout Crisis: A Public Health Problem and the Role of School-Based Health Care," September 6, 2011. www.schoolbasedhealthcare.org.

- **Thirty-four percent** of teen mothers do not go on to earn a high school diploma or GED, according to a 2012 report by America's Promise Alliance.

- A 2010 CBS report found that **half** of all students in the nation's biggest school districts fail to get a high school diploma.

- According to the Philadelphia Public Schools in 2012, only **35 percent** of the city's high school dropouts had a job.

Hispanic Dropout Rate Higher than Others

According to a 2011 US Department of Education report, the high school dropout population is highest among Hispanic youth, with Hispanic males representing the largest group. The statistics indicate the percentage of sixteen- to twenty-four-year-olds who were not enrolled in high school and who lacked a high school credential as of October 2009.

Dropout Rates, by race, ethnicity, and gender, October 2009

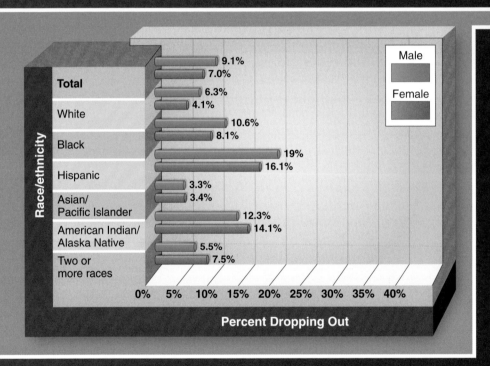

Source: The National Center for Education Statistics, "Trends in High School Dropout and Completion Rates in the United States: 1972–2009, Compendium Report," U.S. Department of Education, October 2011. http://nces.ed.gov.

- The dropout rate for minority students in 2012 was as high as **45 to 50 percent**, according to *THE Journal*.

- As of 2011 Chicago dropouts between age thirteen and twenty-one would fill every seat of the **sixty-one-thousand-capacity Soldier Field**.

Why Do Teens Drop Out of School?

66There was just nothing that was interesting in 10th grade, except my science class. The teacher actually seemed to connect with us. But that was it. And it sure wasn't enough to keep me from dropping.99

—Nate Larson, a Minneapolis dropout.

66Schools still operate with antiquated factory-model, warehouse structures, where 3,000 or more students cycle through six overcrowded classes a day taught by teachers who see far too many students a day to provide them personalized attention.99

—Linda Darling-Hammond, a professor of education at Stanford University.

With statistics clearly illustrating the many problems high school dropouts face throughout their lives, it may seem strange that so many teens continue to make the decision to leave school. In many cases a principal or guidance counselor will follow up with a dropout, asking why he or she has taken that step. Sometimes the responses are clear; other times, students may not know exactly why school is not working for them—only that it is not.

The biggest single reason that girls drop out of high school is pregnancy. Nearly one-third of all girls who drop out of high school list pregnancy or parenthood as the main reason. Though the pregnancy rate among teens in general has dropped since 2001, there are some notable racial and ethnic differences. For example, according to the Guttmacher Institute, which researches reproduction statistics worldwide, the pregnancy rates for black and Hispanic teens in the United States may be as many as two to three times that of white teens. This might help explain why female black and Hispanic teens have higher dropout rates than other racial or ethnic groups.

> **As of 2012 the United States had the highest teen birthrate in the developed world.**

A 2012 report by the National Campaign to Prevent Teen and Unplanned Pregnancy found what many educators and counselors have long suspected—that teen pregnancy and academic failure are closely connected. A pregnant teen is far less likely ever to graduate from high school than a girl who does not get pregnant. The report notes that the likelihood of a pregnant teen graduating from high school is only 51 percent, compared with 89 percent of female students who did not give birth as a teen.

As of 2012 the United States had the highest teen birthrate in the developed world, with approximately 750,000 pregnancies among teens each year. At the same time more than 1 million teens are dropping out of school each year in the United States, and experts see the two problems as closely related.

Trying to Balance School and Pregnancy

Though many girls intend to remain in school to get their diplomas, most find balancing schoolwork and the physical demands of pregnancy far more difficult than they expected. Many are overwhelmed by physical fatigue and end up missing a lot of school. Because they miss more classes, they get further behind, and many drop out as a result. About 70 percent of teens who decide to drop out because of pregnancy do so before the birth of the baby.

After she learned she was pregnant in tenth grade, South Dakota teen Arlyss Harkness promised her mother she would continue with school.

Although she insists that she went as often as she could, she slept late most mornings because she was tired, and she missed a lot of classes. By her fifth month of pregnancy, Harkness had missed too many classes to keep up with her fellow tenth graders. Says Harkness:

> It got to where when I did go, I didn't know what [the class] was doing, and I couldn't catch up. It's like I had no energy. I didn't want to keep showing up and be the dumbest one in the class, just sitting there not knowing what they were talking about. And I felt they were always looking at me, like how could I be so stupid to get pregnant. I was always a pretty good student before that, but this was really humiliating, so I finally just told my advisor I was leaving.[18]

Though she promised her mother that she would return to school or get her GED once the baby was born, Harkness admits that has not happened. "I know it's been almost three years," she says. "But now I'm working part-time to support my child, and I have no time for school. I really do want to finish. I just don't see how it's going to happen."[19]

Family Finances Can Cause Disruption

Another frequently cited reason for a student dropping out is family financial troubles. For example, when a parent is laid off from his or her job, there are severe ramifications for the family's finances. Many families who are unable to keep up with rent or mortgage payments are forced to move.

One counselor says that in many such cases, the school is often the last to know when a student's family moves. Though attendance workers try to contact the family to find out the student's status, they frequently find the phone is disconnected and the house is in foreclosure. "The student may register in another school, in another district," she says. "But there are many times we would never get a request for records for that student, so they might have dropped out permanently. You find yourself wondering what became of him or her, and you do feel badly. You just don't know."[20]

In many households—especially in a bad economy—earning money becomes a family effort, rather than falling only to the parents. An event such as a parent getting injured, diagnosed with a long-term illness, or laid off from a job might lead to a teen dropping out to take a job. "Some families are really on the edge," explains Sandra Ransel, a high school principal in North Las Vegas, Nevada. "They depend on the group to keep them afloat. If they have a younger teen who can work, they sometimes make that choice."[21]

Part-Time Challenges

Cindy Pena was sixteen years old when her mother went through a divorce. The teen began working part-time to help out when her mother was having emotional problems. Cindy initially intended to stay in school while working the extra hours, but she soon learned that to get those hours she had to be flexible about her schedule. And because her mother was having difficulty finding a job, Cindy realized that the only answer was to drop out of school. "Work had to come before school,"[22] she says.

> One counselor says that in many such cases, the school is often the last to know when a student's family moves.

The difficulty of staying in school while working affects even those students who work part-time, just a few days a week. A 2009 survey released by the Boys & Girls Clubs of America found that 32 percent of teens who had left high school admitted that getting a job to support themselves or their families was the biggest obstacle they had faced in completing school.

Ransel has seen firsthand the difficulty teens experience trying to balance a job and schoolwork. "It's very difficult to get up for a 7 a.m. class if you were working until 10 p.m. the night before," she says. "Once kids are spending almost as much time at work as they are in school, it competes. Something usually has to give."[23]

Peer Pressure and Gangs

Education experts say that many teens (and even preteens) are motivated to drop out of school because they belong to gangs. According to the FBI, an estimated 1 million teens and young adults in the United States are members of gangs, especially in larger cities. "The two things [gangs and dropping out] go together," explains Fernando Torres, a member of the grassroots group LA Voice, which tries to empower Los Angeles communities. "Kids look at gangs, and it's like, 'That looks cool and interesting. I'm going to get in, 'cause I want to fit in.' And once they do, they drop out."[24]

In addition to being part of the gang, the lure of easy money selling drugs or engaging in other criminal activities offers a far quicker payoff than any part-time job after school. The money, plus having friends that have dropped out, too, can make leaving school an easy decision. In his book *Dropping Out: Why Students Drop Out of High School and What Can Be Done About It*, Russell W. Rumberger notes that as early as seventh grade, "the most consistent finding is that having deviant friends who have dropped out increases the odds of dropping out."[25]

> " The difficulty of staying in school while working affects even those students who work part-time. "

Patrick Lundvick, a former Chicago gang member, would not disagree with that statement. Growing up poor on the city's South Side, he dropped out of school at age fifteen. He made his living selling drugs and consequently was arrested and spent time in jail. Asked about his decision to leave school, Lundvick explains that it was simply a spur-of-the-moment idea based on the fact that his friends had dropped out. "You think, 'All right, well, my friends are doing it, so I'm going to do it.'"[26]

Fear and Bullying

Sometimes the reason for dropping out comes not from a family or peer group issue, but from within the school. An increasing number of dropouts cite concerns about their personal safety as a reason they stop going to school. According to the teen activism site Do Something, one out of nine high school students, or 2.8 million students, reported that they have been pushed, shoved, tripped, or even spit on during the school year. Another 1.5 million have been threatened with physical harm. Many students who are the targets of bullying or physical threats end up either changing schools or dropping out of school altogether.

Some teens were harassed on the bus on their way to or from school, and others endured bullying in the hallways or lunchroom. The Do Something study found that as many as 57 percent of bullying victims do not bother to report the harassment, because they feel that the teacher or staff member cannot do anything to stop the bullying. Monica, age fifteen, says that she was terrified going to her north Minneapolis school in ninth grade. "I'd get picked on, because of my weight," she says. "It wasn't just boys; it was girls, too, and some of them were as heavy as me. My mom kept saying I should tell my teacher, but [the teacher] never did anything. She was nice, but all us kids knew that she was as scared of [the bullies] as I was."[27]

> "Some teens were harassed on the bus on their way to or from school, and others endured bullying in the hallways or lunchroom.

According to the Do Something study, as many as 10 percent of students who left school before graduating say that being bullied was a key reason that they dropped out. Such statistics are upsetting to US secretary of education Arne Duncan, who says that the suffering endured by those who remain in school is inexcusable and that it is a problem that needs to be addressed quickly. "A school where children don't feel safe is a school where children struggle to learn," he says. "It is a school where kids drop out, tune out, and get depressed. Not just violence but bullying, verbal harassment, substance abuse, cyber-bullying, and disruptive classrooms all interfere with a student's ability to learn."[28]

Disengaged and Uninterested

Education experts say that some of the most common reasons for dropping out are less specific and often more difficult for a dropout to describe. For example, many students are unable to generate the motivation to work hard in school, do the homework assigned by their teachers, or even attend regularly. As one Chicago middle school teacher explains, "It sometimes seems like the kids see no purpose in the things we are teaching them."[29]

The Education Commission of the States is a nonprofit organization whose focus is public education. Jennifer Dounay Zinth, a policy analyst for the commission, believes that her research provides real answers about why so many students drop out before they finish high school. "Students are bored and disengaged," she reports. "Students see no relationship between what they are expected to learn and their future goals. Particularly in large high schools, students say they feel no adult in the building cares about them."[30]

No one answer can explain why more than 1 million teens quit high school each year. But it is clear that unless changes take place, the disturbing dropout rate in the United States will not diminish anytime soon.

Primary Source Quotes*

Why Do Teens Drop Out of School?

66 **Contrary to popular belief, many students do not leave school because too much is expected of them.** 99

—Pennsylvania State Education Association, "Reduce the High School Dropout Rate," PSEA's 20/20 Vision for the Future, 2012. www.psea.org.

The PSEA is an organization of teachers, administrators, and educational support personnel in Pennsylvania's public schools.

66 **The unintended consequence of raising high school graduation requirements has been the skyrocketing of the high school dropout rate.** 99

—James C. Wilson, "Crime and High School Graduation Requirements," *San Diego Union-Tribune*, August 9, 2012. www.utsandiego.com.

Wilson managed career technical education programs for thirty years and has a doctorate in education from the University of Southern California.

Bracketed quotes indicate conflicting positions.

* Editor's Note: While the definition of a primary source can be narrowly or broadly defined, for the purposes of Compact Research, a primary source consists of: 1) results of original research presented by an organization or researcher; 2) eyewitness accounts of events, personal experience, or work experience; 3) first-person editorials offering pundits' opinions; 4) government officials presenting political plans and/or policies; 5) representatives of organizations presenting testimony or policy.

“At-risk students and parents need to be identified in kindergarten and first grade. Parents need to be required to attend classes that teach them how to parent and support their children, as well as inform them of school programs and policies. These classes should not be optional, and sanctions should be put on those who do not comply.”

—Gloria Alkire, "To Address Dropouts, Parents Must Be Part of the Solution," *USA Today*, May 25, 2010. www.usatoday.com.

Alkire has been a teacher and leader in urban schools for more than thirty years.

“Blaming low-income parents for their children's academic woes marginalizes them and further alienates them from a school culture they might already consider unapproachable.”

—Pedro A. Noguera, "Urban Schools Must Start Empowering—and Stop Blaming—Parents," *In Motion Magazine*, June 1, 2011.

Noguera is Peter L. Agnew Professor of Education at New York University.

“We don't really want to face the truth. The truth is far too many California high schools are terrible.”

—James C. Wilson, "Crime and High School Graduation Requirements," August 9, 2012, *San Diego Union-Tribune*. www.utsandiego.com.

Wilson managed career technical education programs for thirty years and has a doctorate in education from the University of Southern California.

“The student who says classes were boring might be signaling a desire for more hands-on learning, a need for more challenging material, or a possible learning disability.”

—Sandra Ransel, "Helping Dropouts Drop Back In," *Educational Leadership*, February 2010. www.ascd.org.

Ransel is the principal of a Las Vegas alternative school for dropouts, Desert Rose High School.

66 Today . . . the public education system remains largely designed to accommodate the average to above-average academic student. 99

—Diane Spencer, participant in *The Forum* (blog), Learning Matters, "Discuss: How Do We Best Prevent Dropouts?," April 21, 2012. http://learningmatters.tv.

Spencer is the student support advocate at Park View Education Centre in Nova Scotia, Canada.

66 Not only is it more likely that kids with learning disabilities are going to drop out of school. It's also less likely they're going to reengage in education. 99

—Tom Hehir, participant in "Engaging Students with Learning Differences Early On," *PBS NewsHour*, PBS, March 21, 2012. www.pbs.org.

Hehir is a professor at the Harvard Graduate School of Education.

66 There's nothing to draw a kid in, nothing to keep them there because everything seems to be shifting under their feet. . . . My first semester of school, one kid said to me, 'Why should I care what you have to say? You won't be here next year.' 99

—David Tanzi, interviewed by Michel Martin, "Teachers Open Up on Why Kids Really Drop Out," NPR, June 14, 2012. www.npr.org.

Tanzi is a math teacher at Dunbar High School in Washington, DC.

Why Do Teens Drop Out of School?

- A 2009 Civic Enterprises report found that **62 percent** of teachers believed a key reason for the high dropout rate was that so many students were unprepared for high school work.

- According to a 2012 Youth Risk Survey in Beloit, Wisconsin, **49 percent** of students said bullying and harassment was a problem at their schools.

- **Forty percent** of teenaged Hispanic girls who drop out do so because they are **pregnant**, according to a National Public Radio report.

- Education expert Robert Balfanz finds that if a sixth grader is absent 20 percent or more of the time, there is a **75 percent** he or she will later drop out.

- In 2011 one-fifth of **dropout factories** were located in rural areas.

- According to a 2010 speech by secretary of education Arne Duncan, one out of nine secondary school students say they were **threatened with harm** during the school year.

- **Sixty-one percent** of teachers and **45 percent** of principals saw lack of support at home as a factor in most cases of students dropping out, according to a 2009 study by Civic Enterprises.

Why Students Drop Out

Experts say there are many reasons why students drop out of school. The Center for Education and Study of Diverse Populations (CESDP) recently reported on the results of a study that asked dropouts why they left school. The report shows a wide variety of explanations but among the most common reasons given are lack of motivation to work hard in school and parents who waited too long before intervening in their child's education.

Reasons Students Drop Out

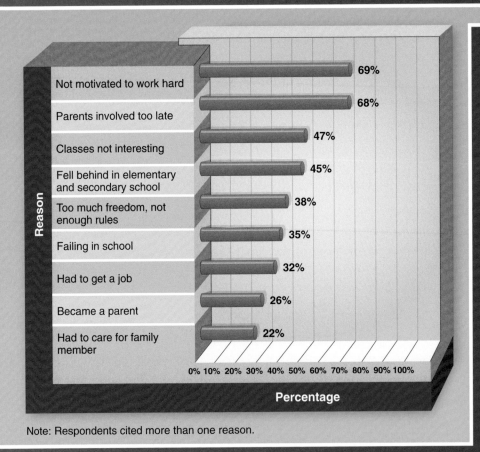

Reason	Percentage
Not motivated to work hard	69%
Parents involved too late	68%
Classes not interesting	47%
Fell behind in elementary and secondary school	45%
Too much freedom, not enough rules	38%
Failing in school	35%
Had to get a job	32%
Became a parent	26%
Had to care for family member	22%

Note: Respondents cited more than one reason.

Source: Center for the Education and Study of Diverse Populations (CESDP), "Gear Up for Students and Parents: Dropout Prevention," New Mexico Highlands University. www.cesdp.nmhu.edu.

Pressures That Lead Pregnant Teens to Drop Out

Pregnancy is the single largest reason for female students to drop out of high school. Among the reasons pregnant teens give for leaving school are morning sickness, insecurity about their changing physical appearance, and lack of encouragement to stay in school.

- Dealing with morning sickness and other side effects of pregnancy
- Feeling insecure about their changing appearance
- Stigmas against pregnant teens from their peers as well as teachers, administrators, and other students' parents
- Being subjected to bullying or sexual harassment
- Inadequate support or encouragement to stay in school
- Lack of day care after the baby is born
- Needing to find a job to support their new baby
- Multiple pregnancies during their teen years

Source: Pregnant Teen Help, "Teen Pregnancy and Facts," November 23, 2010. www.pregnantteenhelp.org.

- A Department of Education study published in 2011 found that high school students from **low-income families** drop out at six times the rate of those from high-income families.

- A 2009 study by the National Assessment of Educational Progress found that only about **30 percent** of incoming high school freshmen could read proficiently.

- According to the National Center for Learning Disabilities in 2012, **20 percent** of teens with learning disabilities drop out of high school each year, compared with **8 percent** of the general population.

Chronic Absenteeism Is a Warning Sign

One early warning sign of a student who is at risk of dropping out is chronic absenteeism. In a 2010 study, researchers in Baltimore, Maryland, tracked absences of students who had missed more than twenty days in ninth grade, and in each of the three years prior to ninth grade. The results show a marked pattern of absences among students who eventually dropped out of school as compared with students who graduated.

Percentage of Students Missing More than Twenty Days of School in First Ninth Grade Year and Three Years Prior, by 2008–09 Outcome

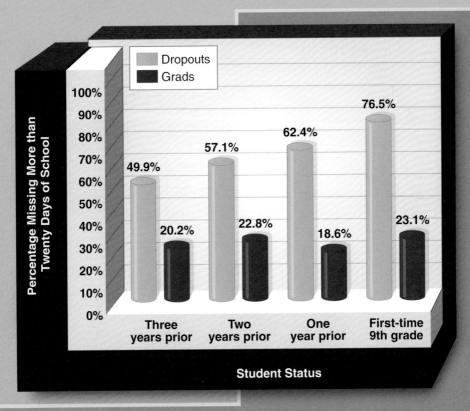

Source: The Baltimore Education Research Consortium, "Gradual Disengagement: A Portrait of the 2008–09 Dropouts in the Baltimore City Schools," 2010. http://baltimore-berc.gov.

Can the Dropout Rate Be Reduced?

> **Trying to reduce the rate of high school dropouts without directly and actively engaging parents is like trying to fix a leaky roof without plugging up the holes.**
>
> —Bill Jackson, founder and CEO of GreatSchools, an independent organization that inspires parents to become involved in their children's education.

> **Every day, this is what I love coming to school for—doing projects and building stuff for the community.**
>
> —James, a high school student and former dropout risk in Fowler United School District.

Gabe, who just turned seventeen, knows he will be older than the others in his tenth-grade class. He was held back in fourth grade because he was having difficulty reading, and he had to repeat the grade. Even with that extra year, however, he continues to have difficulty with some of his core classes, such as math and English. Truancy, he admits, has been another problem for him. He says he hates school and tends to skip classes he does not like—especially English. "I just don't like sitting there every day, trying to pay attention," he says. "None of [the subjects] are that interesting to me, so I just take off. And if I'm being real honest, I don't really know what they're talking about a lot of the time. But when I skip, the attendance office calls my mom, and she gets real mad at me. But I can't help it. I'm not good at school, and I don't like it."[31]

Students like Gabe are likely to drop out. They are uninterested and unmotivated by school. Their classes might seem too difficult or to have little meaning for their future lives.

Education experts know that it is challenging to turn a potential dropout around and make him or her value school and the work it requires. However, some experts believe that the chances of reducing the dropout rate are far better if teachers and school guidance counselors can identify which students are most at risk—and the earlier the better. Over the past decades, researchers have conducted hundreds of studies to find a set of predictors that can identify students who may be on the path to quitting school.

Some of these predictors have to do with a student's academic progress—going as far back as elementary school. For example, a student who has to repeat a grade is a likely candidate for dropping out of school later on. Other predictors are failing important classes like English or math, missing more than twenty days of class during the school year, and chronic misbehavior. According to the American Psychological Association, a child who grows up in poverty is five times more likely to drop out of school than a child growing up in a high-income family.

> "A student who has to repeat a grade is a likely candidate for dropping out of school later on."

Experts stress that such predictors are not causes of dropping out, but rather characteristics that many dropouts share. Recognizing one or more of these predictors in a student can identify someone who may be on the road to dropping out. According to Robert Balfanz, a senior research fellow at Johns Hopkins University, a school's most important challenge occurs once at-risk students are identified. "The fact is that kids don't wake up one day in ninth grade and just quit school," he says. "Instead, that process starts long before, and research shows it's possible to stop it with the right support."[32]

Helping At-Risk Students

Education researchers have seen positive results in Washington, DC, a city whose 58 percent high school graduation rate is among the lowest in the nation. Notes Balfanz, "These high schools educate the highest concentration of students who arrive as ninth graders already significantly off track for high school graduation."[33] Balfanz and others at Johns Hopkins University have developed what they hope is a model for reversing the path of potential dropouts. Called Diplomas Now, the model is based on research showing that a sixth grader demonstrating even one of the dropout predictors has a 75 percent chance of dropping out later on. One of the most promising experiments took place during the 2010–2011 school year at Washington, DC's, Browne Education Campus, which serves students from prekindergarten to eighth grade.

The school used Diplomas Now data to identify at-risk students and tailor individualized plans that could help each one succeed. For example, a student who needed more one-on-one help with reading or math could have a specified time with a tutor built in to his or her schedule. To augment the plans, the school was given extra staff from City Year, a volunteer program for young adults. The volunteers were at school every morning to welcome students, track them down if they did not show up, and tutor any student who needed extra help. Browne was also provided with case managers who could help needy students access resources within their communities.

> The growing dropout rate is not just a problem in large metropolitan high schools.

Browne's results were impressive. After the school year, 38 percent fewer students received school suspensions. And many fewer students failed math and English. The most impressive statistic was Browne's 83 percent reduction in students who had been previously identified as chronically absent. As of 2012 two dozen other schools have partnered with Diplomas Now, hoping to achieve the same positive results.

Coaching Rural Dropout Risks

The growing dropout rate is not just a problem in large metropolitan high schools. Many small rural school districts are fighting the same battles, trying to reverse the growing dropout rate. One such district is in Oconee County, South Carolina, in the foothills of the Appalachian Mountains. The most troubled of the county's high schools, West-Oak, graduates only 71 percent of its seniors. School officials have made an effort to change those numbers. Principal Scott M. Smith used federal stimulus money to pay for specially trained graduation coaches. Their job was to make sure that students showed up for school each day and to provide extra help in subjects that were especially troublesome.

One of the coaches hired by the principal at West-Oak was former math teacher Kevin Burnette. He began by identifying seventy-six at-risk seniors, using frequent absenteeism, failing marks in at least one class, and the failing of any part of the state's high school exit exam as predictors. Burnette explains that many of the at-risk seniors had an unrealistic view of what they could accomplish by dropping out. "I stressed to them that getting a high school diploma opens up the options," he says. "Working for your dad in construction sounds good right now, but five years down the road, you might like to do something else."[34]

> "Service learning for Fowler's high school students involved helping immigrants prepare for their upcoming citizenship test."

Though he connected with many of his clients, Burnette was disappointed that eleven of them ended up dropping out. In the future he would like to begin coaching students earlier than their senior year. "I'd like to begin working more with our 9th grade students," he says, "to help them understand how important a high school diploma is."[35]

Making School Interesting

Some districts are trying to reduce the dropout rate by adding school projects that motivate students to attend more regularly. One that has drawn attention in recent years is service learning, which combines community involvement with classroom learning. In 2000 superintendent John Cruz of the California Valley's Fowler Unified School District decided to try service learning as a way to combat the high dropout rate in his district. In Fresno County, where the Fowler District is located, about one in three young people who started ninth grade failed to graduate four years later. The largely Hispanic population ranges from very poor to middle class.

Cruz first started the children volunteering in elementary school; some tended the school's garden, while others hatched trout eggs that would later be released into the San Joaquin River to help a depleted fish population. Service learning for Fowler's high school students involved helping immigrants prepare for their upcoming citizenship test. The students did more than merely show up to help; they spent class time learning about the work they would be doing. That means that younger children learned about the life cycle of fish or the proper way to care for growing vegetables. Those helping recent immigrants learned more not only about the topics covered in the citizenship test, but also about the cultural and ethnic backgrounds of the people they would be helping.

> **Many students who drop out at age sixteen or seventeen have serious learning problems.**

Due to the high student interest in such projects, Cruz's service learning curriculum has made a noticeable difference in the district's dropout rates. Ten years after starting the program, the district's average attendance rate had jumped to an unprecedented 97 percent, while the dropout rate fell to less than 1 percent. A study of the program by Civic Engagement, a public-policy firm in Washington, DC, found that even students who were not usually eager about school projects were enthusiastic about being involved in service learning.

Is College the Only Goal?

Many US high schools focus their efforts on preparing students for four-year colleges and universities. Often college is seen as the only worthwhile outcome of a high school diploma. However, experts point out that this route might not be right for every student. For some high school graduates, trade school, vocational school, or a two-year junior college program might be more appropriate.

In standardizing curricula for college-bound students, says Stanford University education professor Nel Noddings, high schools are losing students who have no interest in classes such as Shakespearean literature or advanced geometry and who cannot see a connection between such subjects and their future job possibilities. Noddings suggests that high schools could reduce dropout numbers and better prepare students for life after high school by offering other types of classes to students who might not be interested in college. She writes:

It is politically incorrect today to suggest that some kids have neither the interest or the aptitude for academic mathematics. Nevertheless, it is true. When I taught high school math (everything from general math to Advanced Placement calculus), I was continually astonished at the range of achievement that appeared in every course. It was wonderful to work with kids who were eager to learn more and more. But it was also gratifying to help less interested students find material connected to their own purposes. . . . There are many intelligent, industrious, morally decent, creative people who dislike academic math and really don't need it.[36]

Changing the Age Requirement

One controversial idea for reducing the dropout rate is to raise the age requirement for students to stay in school. As of 2012 twenty-one states require students to remain in school until they turn eighteen or graduate, while in twenty-nine states, students may legally drop out of school at seventeen, or with parental permission, at sixteen. Educators who support raising the age requirement say that it will encourage teens to stay in school and avoid an immature decision that could haunt them years later. They also hope that by being required to attend longer, students may be inspired to pursue further study, perhaps at a community college.

In his 2012 State of the Union address to a joint session of Congress, Barack Obama challenged all fifty states to legally prevent students from quitting school before age eighteen. "When students aren't allowed to walk away from their education," Obama said, "more of them walk the stage to get their diploma."[37]

Not everyone agrees with the president's idea. Many students who drop out at age sixteen or seventeen have serious learning problems. One concern is that forcing them to remain in school could increase behavior problems and interfere with the learning of more-interested students. Many agree with education expert William Berkson of the Jewish Institute for Youth and Family, who notes that such students "cannot follow the lessons, and so they are bored, and more importantly, humiliated by their inabilities."[38]

Money is also a concern. Usually, such students need more individualized help, including remedial courses and counseling. State Senator Kimberly Lightford, the head of the Illinois Senate's Education Committee, worries about the economic burden the president's plan would put upon an already strained budget for Chicago's public schools. She wonders, "Where are we going to get the money?"[39]

No Quick Fixes

While some of the ideas currently in use to reduce the dropout rate hold promise, experts acknowledge that there is no one answer to the growing problem. Schools and the populations they serve differ in economic status, the value the community puts on education, and even the number of parent volunteers who can assist in the classroom. It seems, however, that the best remedy for the growing dropout problem is a combination of strong parent involvement, a supportive peer group, and school budgets for hiring additional teachers and counselors.

Can the Dropout Rate Be Reduced?

66 Instead of defining success solely in terms of mastering a college-preparatory curriculum, we should develop a broader measure of high school success, one that includes vocational and technical education as well as the arts and humanities. 99

—Russell W. Rumberger, *Dropping Out: Why Students Drop Out of High School and What Can Be Done About It.* Cambridge, MA: Harvard University Press, 2011.

Rumberger is a professor of education at the University of California–Santa Barbara.

66 I have to point out, in the 21st century, high schools shouldn't just make sure students graduate—they should make sure students graduate ready for college, ready for a career, and ready for life. 99

—Barack Obama, "Remarks by the President at the America's Promise Alliance Education Event," March 1, 2010. www.whitehouse.gov.

Obama is the forty-fourth president of the United States.

* Editor's Note: While the definition of a primary source can be narrowly or broadly defined, for the purposes of Compact Research, a primary source consists of: 1) results of original research presented by an organization or researcher; 2) eyewitness accounts of events, personal experience, or work experience; 3) first-person editorials offering pundits' opinions; 4) government officials presenting political plans and/or policies; 5) representatives of organizations presenting testimony or policy.

"We continue to insist that, like it or not, all children should be prepared for college so that they will have a chance at a more affluent life. The purpose of education has been reduced to making money. What about liking one's work?"

—Nel Noddings, "Differentiate, Don't Standardize," *Education Week*, January 7, 2010. www.edweek.org.

Noddings is the Lee L. Jacks Professor of Education Emerita at Stanford University.

"Florida was among the first to require high school majors statewide. While somewhat controversial, the move has proved successful at getting students to leave high school the right way—as a graduate rather than a dropout."

—Caroline Cournoyer, "High School Majors Help Some States Cut Dropout Rate," Governing, August 2012. www.governing.com.

Cournoyer is deputy web officer for the website Governing and has written for *Teacher* magazine.

"If we want kids to graduate from high school, then having a strong foundation at the elementary level is critical. And for kids with significant learning disabilities and significant attention-deficit disorders, having technologies, providing accommodations for reading and writing are critical."

—Tom Hehir, participant in "Engaging Students with Learning Differences Early On," *PBS NewsHour*, PBS, March 21, 2012. www.pbs.org.

Hehir is a professor at the Harvard Graduate School of Education.

"That sense of shepherding is what the kids need, to know that an adult not only cares, but the adult can actually help them."

—Robert Balfanz, interviewed by *Frontline*, "Middle School Moment," PBS, July 17, 2012. www.pbs.org.

Balfanz is a senior research scientist at Johns Hopkins University.

"Many reformers focus their dropout prevention efforts on high schoolers; replacing large high schools with smaller learning communities where poor students can get individualized instruction from dedicated teachers has been shown to be effective."

—Henry M. Levin and Cecilia E. Rouse, "The True Cost of High School Dropouts," *New York Times*, January 25, 2012. www.nytimes.com.

Levin is a professor of economics and education at Teachers College, Columbia University; Rouse is a professor of economics and public affairs at Princeton University.

"Some Americans probably think that preventing 1.3 million students from dropping out of high school can't be done—but in fact the costs of inaction are far greater."

—Henry M. Levin and Cecilia E. Rouse, "The True Cost of High School Dropouts," *New York Times*, January 25, 2010. www.nytimes.com.

Levin is a professor of economics and education at Teachers College, Columbia University; Rouse is a professor of economics and public affairs at Princeton University.

"One can't really address the drop-out crisis without making school much more engaging for low-income teenagers, whether or not they show an inclination toward making it to and through a four-year college."

—Dana Goldstein, "Scratching the Surface of Obama's Education Rhetoric," *Nation*, January 25, 2012. www.thenation.com.

Goldstein is a columnist for the *Nation*.

"To reduce boredom and disengagement, states might consider expanding opportunities for project-based and hands-on learning."

—Jennifer Dounay Zinth, participant in "Discuss: How Do We Best Prevent Dropouts?," *The Forum* (blog), Learning Matters, April 21, 2012. http://learningmatters.tv.

Zinth codirects the Education Commission of the States Information Clearinghouse, which provides police and research information to education leaders.

Can the Dropout Rate Be Reduced?

- A 2009 survey by Civic Enterprises found that **75 percent** of teachers believed that smaller classes would help reduce the dropout rate.

- According to America's Promise Alliance, disadvantaged children can arrive at kindergarten already **eighteen months behind**—something that good early childhood education, such as Head Start, can prevent.

- Between 2000 and 2009 the Bill & Melinda Gates Foundation invested more than **$2 billion** to redesign existing high schools or create new high schools to make dropping out less likely for at-risk students.

- In August 2011 New York City mayor Michael Bloomberg and billionaire George Soros donated **$200 million** to a number of initiatives aimed at helping stem poor academic performance, a skyrocketing rate of suspensions, and high numbers of dropouts among African American and Hispanic youth.

- More than **75 percent** of teachers and **71 percent** of principals strongly favored making alternative learning environments available within high schools to make sure all students graduate, according to a 2009 Civic Enterprises report.

- The number of **dropout factories** shrank from 2,007 in 2002 to 1,550 in 2010, according to the report "Building a Grad Nation" in 2012.

How Educators Would Lower the Dropout Rate

Principals and teachers have strong ideas about ways to lower the US dropout rate. An *Education Week* article that examines educators' views of the dropout problem highlights a survey in which teachers and principals cite the measures they believe would reduce the number of students who drop out of school.

Measures educators say would reduce the rate of student dropouts:

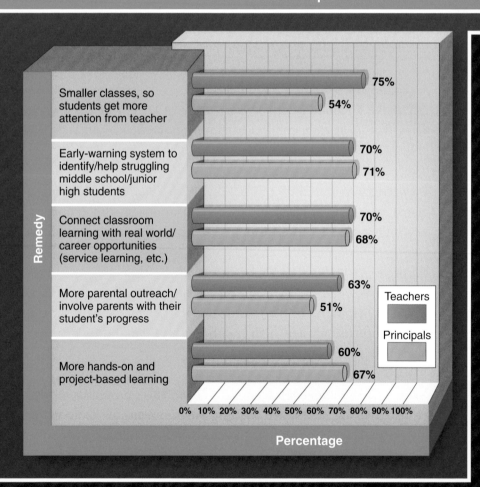

Source: Catherine Gewertz, "Schism on Dropout Problem Seen," *Education Week*, June 10, 2009, p.12.

Academic Dropout Factories Declining

Educators agree that dropout factories—high schools that graduate fewer than 60 percent of their students—are responsible for many dropouts. According to the 2012 update to the "Building a Grad Nation" report, in the years from 2002 to 2010, school districts have improved or closed 23 percent of dropout factories.

Graduation Year	Total Number of High Schools with a Graduation Rate of 60% or below
Class of 2002	2,007
Class of 2008	1,746
Class of 2009	1,634
Class of 2010	1,550

Source: Civic Enterprises, Everyone Graduates Center, America's Promise Alliance, and the Alliance for Excellent Education, "Building a Grad Nation: Progress and Challenge in Ending the High School Dropout Epidemic," 2012. www.civicenterprises.net.

- One thousand Chicago high school students at risk of not graduating because of missed credits were able to graduate with their class by **making up classes online**, according to Robin Gonzales of Chicago Public Schools.

- Between 2000 and 2010 **thirty-one states** expanded alternatives for graduating students at risk for dropping out, according to a 2010 report from Johns Hopkins University.

- Hoping to reduce its dropout rate, Baltimore, Maryland, adopted a **zero-tolerance policy for truancy** in 2011, by which schools can fine parents fifty dollars or even jail them if their children miss twenty or more days of school.

What Can Be Done to Help Dropouts?

"This is my personal miracle. I am back where I was before I dropped out of high school."

—Charles Griffin, a former dropout from Washington State, who recently earned his GED through the YouthBuild program.

"Six to 12 months ago they were sleeping late. And all of a sudden they're in a cap and gown walking in front of a crowd of people applauding and saying, 'You did it! You did it!'"

—Robert Parker, CEO of NewBridge, a school that helps dropouts earn a high school diploma.

While some experts are focusing their efforts on preventing more teens from dropping out, others are looking for ways to lure back those who already have dropped out. Occasionally, it may not take much convincing, especially if the teen or young adult has had a great deal of difficulty finding a job. But once a student has left school, it is usually more difficult to persuade him or her to return.

Project U-Turn

In Pennsylvania the School District of Philadelphia has been making progress in its efforts to lure dropouts back to school with a program that began in 2006 called Project U-Turn. In 2004 only 49 percent of the city's ninth graders were graduating in four years, with thirty thousand teens leaving school each year without a diploma. By 2011, thanks in large part to Project U-Turn, the city's graduation rate had jumped 12 percentage points to 61 percent.

Under Project U-Turn, reenrollment centers operate throughout the district. They are staffed by counselors who meet with teens who want to learn more about returning to school for a diploma. Counselors work with those teens to address their needs for affordable child care, extra help with a learning problem, and other issues that might prevent them from going back to school. In addition, Project U-Turn can help returning teens find affordable health care and match them with people in the workforce who can answer career questions.

Laura Shubilla, president of the Philadelphia Youth Network, has been credited with the massive effort to bring dropouts back to schools. She believes that making a commitment to educate even the most difficult-to-reach youth demonstrates a community's strength. "If you can do this right and pull this off," she says, "not only is it an economic imperative locally and nationally, but just the moral imperative of it becomes very powerful for a city."[40]

"We Want You Back" Day

In Rochester, Minnesota, volunteers have decided not to wait for dropouts to seek help in returning to school. In the fall of 2012, Rochester Public Schools and the United Way of Olmsted County announced that October 6 would be "We Want You Back" Day. Armed with data about the financial effects of dropping out and the difficulties that dropouts are likely to experience, teams of community volunteers planned to go door-to-door to homes of high school students who dropped out over the summer.

Officials estimated that about two hundred students would be visited. The volunteers planned to assess why each dropout decided to leave and what was necessary to bring him or her back to school. "I hope to be on one of those volunteer teams," says Mary Jorgens, whose son dropped out in eleventh grade several years ago. "He finally went back for his high school diploma, but in the meantime, he had a rough three years unemployed. That was time he could have spent learning a trade. At this age, a

> " Counselors work with those teens to address their needs for affordable child care. "

lot of kids just don't see the big picture, and I hope 'We Want You Back' Day wakes a lot of them up."[41]

The Limits of a GED

A growing number of teen dropouts are learning that finding a job is far more difficult than they had anticipated. Many decide to sign up for a class to get their GED. First introduced after World War II, the GED was intended to help returning veterans—many of whom did not finish high school before enlisting or being drafted—show that they had enough knowledge to get a job or begin college. In the years since then, more than 18 million Americans have obtained a GED rather than a standard high school diploma. According to the American Council on Education, each year about four hundred thousand people pass the GED test.

While for decades the GED was considered to be virtually synonymous with a high school diploma, experts today say the value of the GED has been vastly undermined by a troubled economy. The dropout would be better off returning to a school at which he or she could get a high school diploma, they suggest, or else pair a GED with real work experience that would impress a future employer. "The GED is a credential," says John Deasy, superintendent of the Los Angeles Unified School District. "Is it adequate for gainful employment and a living wage in the United States today? I do not think so."[42]

Education expert Russell W. Rumberger, author of *Dropping Out*, agrees, saying that for a prospective employer, a GED alone is not necessarily a useful tool by which to measure the job candidate. "If you look at employer surveys, the things that employers generally most look for or think are important, especially at lower-end jobs" says Rumberger, "are the things like perseverance and tenacity, and those kinds of qualities that are not measured by the GED."[43]

Different Kinds of Schools

Many educators believe that a high school diploma is the better solution. But for many dropouts, returning to a traditional high school setting is not the answer. Going back to the school that did not work for that student before may be intimidating to a dropout. Too, though the 8 a.m. to 3 p.m. school day may work for the majority of teens, for others who have young children or who work late hours at a job, and especially those who have done poorly in school in the past, a regular high school curriculum will not be a good fit.

For those reasons, many districts have created different types of schools for dropouts who want to get their diplomas. Sometimes called learning centers, they are often smaller than regular high schools but with faculty and facilities that can address the specific needs of the students. For example, learning centers that cater to students who are pregnant or have small children usually feature child care on-site. Other learning centers attract students who are nonnative English speakers and who need intensive help with reading and writing in English. And many such centers have flexible hours to meet the work schedules of returning students. Some are funded by philanthropic organizations, and others are funded through school districts. Most are free or at very low cost to the student.

One alternative high school solely aimed at helping dropouts is Desert Rose in Las Vegas, Nevada. Principal Sandra Ransel explains that the students can achieve success because the school is willing to be flexible. "When we fashion school in ways that meet these students' circumstances," she says, "many dropouts can receive a traditional diploma or general education diploma (GED) in as little as six months and quickly enter the workforce or pursue postsecondary education."[44]

> " Many districts have created different types of schools for dropouts who want to get their diplomas. "

Classes last for three hours, and a student can come in the afternoon or evening, whichever is more convenient. The school has a One Stop Center that helps students with questions about finding child care, tutoring, transportation, and many other issues. It is staffed by volunteers from AmeriCorps, the American Association of Retired Persons, the Urban League, and other agencies and nonprofit organizations.

Desert Rose has had great success since opening in 2001, with twenty-eight hundred students earning diplomas. About 50 percent of the graduates go on to community or four-year colleges. Twenty-five percent work full-time after graduating, and another 25 percent enlist in the military.

YouthBuild

One large program that combines earning a GED or high school diploma with work experience is YouthBuild. It began as an informal project in Harlem, New York, in 1978. A group of teenagers led by teacher Dorothy Stoneman found a way to renovate empty, rundown houses and other buildings that had become havens for drug dealers and other criminals. Not only did their project help improve their community by turning the buildings into affordable housing for residents, but it also provided the teens with a worthwhile learning project with a satisfying conclusion.

Over the years the idea has expanded into forty-six states, as well as Washington, DC, and the Virgin Islands. YouthBuild is funded in part by grants from the US Department of Labor, as well as educational initiatives from community and faith-based organizations. As of 2011 more than one-hundred-ten thousand YouthBuild participants—all lower-income dropouts—have built twenty-one thousand units of affordable housing.

> "Classes last for three hours, and a student can come in the afternoon or evening."

But building is only part of what participants do. Students take classes in mathematics and English, and they are required to do one hundred hours of community service before they are allowed to graduate. Michigan YouthBuild instructor Jeff Doublestein insists that the point is not to prepare students for jobs as builders. "Our whole objective is not to create construction workers," he says. "We want to use construction as a means to instill work ethic into them and also employable skills."[45]

Rebecca Villanueva, who is registered in YouthBuild's San Jose, California, initiative, has gone from jail, to being a homeless dropout and living in her car, to earning her high school diploma. She hopes to go on to college and study criminal justice or psychology. She says that she never envisioned herself as enjoying the kind of success she has had in the program—especially in helping others. "The families we're helping tell us how much they appreciate us, and that's what really affects me,"[46] she says.

Youth ChalleNGe

Another program that has had success with dropouts is the National Guard's Youth ChalleNGe. While YouthBuild combines construction work and schoolwork, Youth ChalleNGe matches a military atmosphere and discipline with high school classes for dropouts between sixteen and eighteen years old.

The program takes place at camps located on military bases at thirty-three locations in twenty-seven states, and Youth ChalleNGe officials say that distance from their neighborhoods is a good thing for many of the teens. "By taking them away from their neighborhoods, we're giving them a safe place to get their act together," says Janet Zimmerman, a retired army colonel who runs a camp at Fort Gordon, Georgia. "These youths have been told they are failures. Here they find that if they straighten up, others will believe in them."[47]

> At the school, former graduates of the program work as 'chasers' to make sure students get to class and have their homework done.

The cadets, as they are called, take regular classes each day, striving either for a GED or high school diploma. In addition, they work on stress and anger management and physical fitness, and they must complete forty hours of community service projects, both individually and within groups. The program, which started in 1993, boasts sixty-four thousand graduates who have earned academic credentials.

Chasing Students

One of the biggest challenges for programs aimed at helping dropouts complete their education is getting the students to show up for classes and do their assignments. Mikala Rahn, who runs an independent school for dropouts in Pasadena, California, has noticed that besides being poor, many of her students are also quite alone in the world. Some are homeless; others are estranged from families. Many have histories of substance abuse or have served time in prison. These types of life experiences are not conducive to completing an education.

In an effort to overcome these challenges, Rahn has instituted a program that helps provide structure and discipline to returning dropouts. Rahn's school, called Learning Works, serves up to three hundred students. At the school, former graduates of the program work as "chasers" to make sure students get to class and have their homework done. One chaser, Dominic Correy, defines his role as a mentor, parent, and alarm clock, adding, "Some people say a truant officer."[48] Carlos Cruz, another chaser explains, "The main goal of everything we do is to eliminate any and every excuse that they can imagine [for] why they are not attempting to achieve their high school diploma."[49]

A Second Chance

Whether dropouts return to education through traditional high schools, federal programs, or small alternative schools, they are trying to regain the promise of an education that previously had been lost. Experts seem to agree that whichever way dropouts reach their goal, the outcome of obtaining a high school diploma does make a difference—not only to the student but to the community as a whole.

What Can Be Done to Help Dropouts?

66 Until this day, I honestly have my diploma in my trunk. It goes with me everywhere I go. For me it was I think the biggest thing I have ever done. 99

—Carlos Cruz, participant in "Former Dropouts Push Others to Reach Finish Line," *NPR Weekend Edition*, June 24, 2012. www.npr.org.

Cruz, a former at-risk teen, works at an alternative school for dropouts, Learning Works, in Pasadena, California.

66 We will have a very highly visible, youth-friendly system for reaching these kids, figuring out what the best fit is for them, and counseling them into those seats. 99

—Jennifer Vidis, participant in Linda Lutton, "Luring Chicago Dropouts Back to School, One Doorstep at a Time," WBEZ91.5 podcast, August 25, 2011. www.wbez.org.

Vidis oversees alternative schools for the Chicago Public Schools.

* Editor's Note: While the definition of a primary source can be narrowly or broadly defined, for the purposes of Compact Research, a primary source consists of: 1) results of original research presented by an organization or researcher; 2) eyewitness accounts of events, personal experience, or work experience; 3) first-person editorials offering pundits' opinions; 4) government officials presenting political plans and/or policies; 5) representatives of organizations presenting testimony or policy.

66 **Three in four students graduating from high school is nothing to celebrate in a country like ours.** 99

—Andrew J. Rotherham, "Dropout Rates Dropping, but Don't Celebrate Yet," *Time*, November 30, 2010. www.time.com.

Rotherham is a cofounder of Bellwether Education, a nonprofit group working to improve educational outcomes for low-income students.

66 **Relationships are essential. Dropouts often drift on a sea of good intentions. They will quickly sign up for classes and dip their toes in the classroom, but if some caring adult does not quickly convince these students that success is possible, they don't stay.** 99

—Sandra Ransel, "Helping Dropouts Drop Back In," *Educational Leadership*, February 2010. www.ascd.org.

Ransel is the principal of a Las Vegas alternative school for dropouts, Desert Rose High School.

66 **It's kind of an oxymoron, but we used an early college philosophy for dropouts. We brought them back in. Our message was, you didn't finish high school. Start college today.** 99

— Daniel King, participant in "In South Texas, Luring Dropouts Back by Sending Them to College," *PBS Newshour*, July 4, 2012. www.pbs.org.

King is the superintendent of the Pharr–San Juan–Alamo School District and participated in the American Graduate program for dropouts.

66 **While teens in mainstream high schools are choosing a dress or tux for prom this month, my students are studying for their exam as parents, ex-offenders transitioning back to society, non-English speakers, and patients combating disease.** 99

—Nakia Hill, "A GED Safety Net for High School Dropouts," *Christian Science Monitor*, April 26, 2012.

Hill teaches a GED class for high school dropouts in Boston, Massachusetts.

❝If I were prepared today with a GED, and that's what I had as an 18-year-old, I'd be scared to death of the future.❞

—Ed Morris, participant in Claudio Sanchez, "In Today's Economy, How Far Can a GED Take You?," *NPR Weekend Edition*, February 18, 2012. www.npr.org.

Morris is the head of Adult and Career Education for Los Angeles Schools.

....

❝The ChalleNGe program provides participants an opportunity to develop the values, skills, education and self-discipline to succeed as responsible citizens.❞

Youth ChalleNGe Program, "2011: Performance and Accountability Highlights, 2011. http://ngycp.org/etc/pdf/NGB2011YouthChallenge_012612.pdf.

The Youth ChalleNGe Program is a program for dropouts created and run by the National Guard.

....

Facts and Illustrations

What Can Be Done to Help Dropouts?

- According to the Early College High School Initiative, as of 2011 there were 240 schools in twenty-eight states that allow high school students to **simultaneously complete a high school diploma and the first two years of college**, helping many youth at risk of dropping out see the value of continuing their education.

- As of 2011 **YouthBuild programs** (helping dropouts by pairing learning construction skills with earning a diploma) exist in forty-five states; Washington, DC; and the Virgin Islands.

- A community center in Oakland, California, that helps dropouts get their GEDs announced in 2012 that **75 percent** of them go on to a community college or a vocational school.

- Hoping to lure dropouts back to school, in 2012 the Las Vegas Latin Chamber of Commerce offered a **five-hundred-dollar** scholarship to any dropout who returns to high school and graduates.

- Youth ChalleNGe, a National Guard program for young people who have dropped out of school, graduated its **one-hundred-thousandth** cadet at the end of 2011.

- According to Youth ChalleNGe officials in 2009, about **20 percent** of cadets opt out of the program—often because of the structure and discipline—usually within the first two weeks.

National Guard Program for Dropouts

The National Guard Youth ChalleNGe Program is a community-based program that leads, trains, and mentors high school dropouts so that they may become productive citizens. According to a 2011 report on the program's accomplishments, a large percentage of Youth ChalleNGe graduates have either continued their education or have found full-time employment.

Graduate Placement Categories

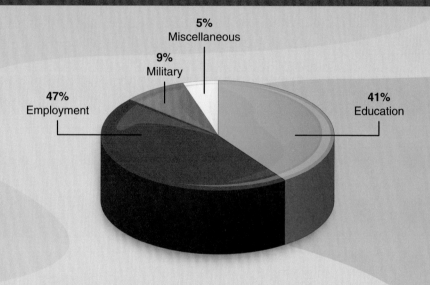

- 5% Miscellaneous
- 9% Military
- 47% Employment
- 41% Education

Note: Due to rounding, numbers may not total 100 percent.

Source: Youth ChalleNGe Program 2011: Performance and Accountability Highlights. http:ngycp.org.

- Each year in the United States, about **seven-hundred-fifty-thousand** dropouts take the GED test.

- Since it began in 2007, the College Career and Technology Academy program in Texas has graduated **eight hundred seventy-eight** students, all former dropouts.

Difficulties in Reconnecting with School

"Opportunity Road" is a project aimed at helping the estimated 6.7 million "opportunity youth"—disadvantaged young people between sixteen and twenty-four who are out of school and out of work. In their January 2012 report, "Opportunity Road: The Promise and Challenge of America's Forgotten Youth," researchers from a consortium of philanthropic organizations wanted to know the obstacles faced by dropouts, so that educators could assist those youth to reconnect more smoothly with school.

Obstacles to Reconnecting to School

This is a big factor in my decision not to attend college or technical school this year:

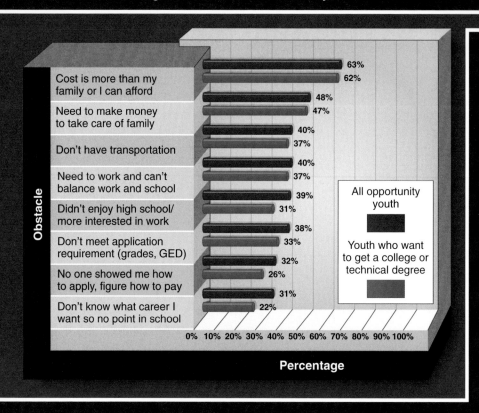

Source: John Bridgeland and Jessica A. Milano, "Opportunity Road: The Promise and Challenge of America's Forgotten Youth," January 2012. www.civicenterprises.net.

- One dropout recovery program, Philadelphia's Re-Engagement Center, enforces a **strict dress code** for the dropouts who attend.

- **Twenty-one percent** of cadets at Youth ChalleNGe are female.

- In an effort to help dropouts transition back to school and get a degree, the United Way announced in August 2012 that it is seeking to recruit **1 million volunteer readers**, tutors, and mentors by 2014.

Key People and Advocacy Groups

America's Promise Alliance: Under the directorship of General Colin Powell and chaired by his wife, Alma Powell, this organization is the largest partnership in the United States dedicated to improving the lives of American youth. The alliance has made the dropout crisis a signature issue.

Robert Balfanz: Codirector of the Everyone Graduates Center and the Center for Social Organization of Schools at Johns Hopkins University, Balfanz was the first to identify predictors of dropping out—including frequent absences, misbehavior, and difficulty with class work. He has published many papers and reports, especially on high school dropouts and schools in high-poverty areas.

City Year: A national service program whose goal is to fight the dropout crisis in the United States. Founded in 1988, City Year's participants act as mentors, tutors, and role models in schools to help students stay on track, or get back on track, so that they can graduate.

Arne Duncan: Secretary of education under Barack Obama, Duncan, a former Chicago Public Schools administrator, has highlighted the dropout problem as a critical issue in public education today. He has also identified school bullying as a contributing factor to the dropout crisis.

Bill and Melinda Gates: The Gateses are philanthropists and cochairs of the Bill & Melinda Gates Foundation, which supports a wide range of educational organizations, including Gateway to College. This program helps dropouts—or those on the path to becoming dropouts—get on track to complete high school and simultaneously earn college credits.

Nel Noddings: The Lee L. Jacks Professor of Education Emerita at Stanford University, Noddings has strong feelings about the changing role of modern schools. To minimize the dropout rate, she believes schools should avoid standardizing their curricula. Instead, offering different types of training and education will allow students having a range of interests and abilities to find a niche in employment.

Nelson Reidar: An educator who has worked for forty-one years in public schools as a teacher and principal, Reidar spent a year working at a California dropout factory. His 2011 book about his experiences, *Education Malpractice: A Year in a Dropout Factory*, illustrates how poverty, lack of interest by many faculty and staff members, and noninvolvement by parents can create a toxic education environment.

Project U-Turn: A program aimed at reclaiming dropouts in Philadelphia, a city where 40 percent of ninth graders fail to graduate within six years. Project U-Turn is a collaborative effort among parents, youth, community and city agencies, the school district, and various organizations that serve young people. Project U-Turn has made the dropout problem the city's number one priority.

YouthBuild: A nonprofit program funded by the Department of Labor that provides education, job skills, and career counseling to high school dropouts. There are more than two hundred seventy-three YouthBuild programs throughout the United States. Enrollees learn basic construction skills and build low-income housing; on alternate weeks they do classroom work toward earning their GED or high school diploma.

Youth ChalleNGe: A program for dropouts run by the National Guard. Youth ChalleNGe targets youth between sixteen and eighteen and combines intensive schoolwork with a military lifestyle for a twenty-two-week period then are mentored for a year. Youth ChalleNGe has had success, with many of its "cadets" earning a diploma or GED, or finding full-time employment after taking part in the program.

Chronology

1940
US Census figures show 44.2 percent of Americans between the ages of twenty and twenty-four had earned a high school diploma.

1964
President Lyndon Johnson urges legislation funding the Neighborhood Youth Corps to help dropouts receive job training while requiring them to stay in school.

1961
US secretary of labor Arthur Goldberg warns teens not to drop out because the job market is becoming more competitive.

1940   1960   1980

1950
The American Council on Education begins offering the GED to returning veterans of World War II and other nongraduates.

1970
US Census figures show that among Americans between the ages of twenty and twenty-four, 79 percent had graduated from high school.

1963
President John F. Kennedy seeks and receives $250,000 in federal funds to hire more counselors to go door-to-door in sixty-three cities to urge dropouts to return to school.

1983
The US government publishes a report called *A Nation at Risk*, calling for more rigorous standards for high school graduates.

Chronology

1988
The City Year program begins, encouraging youth to help mentor, tutor, or otherwise support students who are on a path toward dropping out of school.

2011
Nelson Reidar releases *Education Malpractice: A Year in a Dropout Factory.*

1990
President George H.W. Bush and the governors of all fifty US states adopt six goals for education to be met by 2000—one of which is a 90 percent graduation rate.

2001
President George W. Bush signs into law the No Child Left Behind Act, making states accountable for dropouts.

1990

2000

2010

1994
The US Department of Labor's Youth-Build program for dropouts begins.

2012
President Barack Obama calls for legislation to make all students stay in school until age eighteen.

1993
The National Guard's Youth ChalleNGe Program begins, helping dropouts get on track to continue their education.

2002
Experts at Johns Hopkins University describe schools that graduate fewer than 60 percent of their students as "dropout factories."

Related Organizations

American Youth Policy Forum

1836 Jefferson Place NW
Washington, DC 20036
phone: (202) 775-9731 • fax: (202) 775-9733
website: www.aypf@aypf.org

The American Youth Policy Forum is a nonprofit development organization that provides learning opportunities for policy leaders, practitioners, and researchers working on youth and education issues. The forum has made the dropout crisis one of its main focuses.

City-As-School (CAS)

16 Clarkson St.
New York, NY 10014
phone: (212) 337-6800
website: www.city-as.net

City-As-School is a New York City independent alternative high school program for eleventh- and twelfth-grade students at risk for dropping out. The program combines academic learning with work in local businesses. Students learn in small specialized classes that utilize a range of business, civil, cultural, and political resources.

Communities in Schools

2345 Crystal Dr., Suite 801
Arlington, VA 22202
phone: (800) 247-4543
e-mail: info@cisnet.org • website: www.communitiesinschools.org

Communities in Schools is an organization whose mission is to keep students in school by identifying problems students have and then addressing those problems before they can cause a child to drop out. The organization's workers establish relationships with local businesses, service agencies, and volunteer organizations to provide needed resources for this work.

Related Organizations

Everyone Graduates Center

2701 N. Charles St., Suite 300
Baltimore, MD 21218
phone: (410) 516-8315 • fax: (410) 516-8890
website: www.every1graduates.org

The mission of the Everyone Graduates Center is to develop and disseminate the information necessary to enable all students to graduate from high school. The center works to identify the obstacles that stand in the way of some students graduating and then develops solutions to overcome those obstacles.

Gateway to College

Gateway to College National Network
529 SE Grand Ave., Suite 300
Portland, OR 97214
phone: (971) 634-1212 • fax: (971) 634-1213
website: www.gatewaytocollege.org

Offering a second chance to high school dropouts and those who are on the verge of dropping out, Gateway to College provides a structure within which teens can earn a high school diploma while at the same time earning college credits. The Bill & Melinda Gates Foundation funds the program, which had thirty-three sites in twenty states as of 2012.

National Center for Education Statistics (NCES)

Institute of Education Sciences
1990 K St. NW, 8th and 9th Floors
Washington, DC 20006
phone: (202) 502-7300 • fax: (202) 502-7466
website: http://nces.ed.gov

The NCES is the primary federal entity for collecting, reviewing, and analyzing educational data. The NCES has provided valuable research that enables teachers and policy makers to understand trends in the dropout rate and decide on programs or solutions that may prove helpful in addressing the problem.

National Dropout Prevention Center

Clemson University
209 Martin St.
Clemson, SC 29631-1555
phone: (864) 656-2599 • fax: (864) 656-0136
e-mail: ndpc@clemson.edu • website: www.dropoutprevention.org

The National Dropout Prevention Center was founded in 1986 to serve as a clearinghouse on issues that are related to dropout prevention, as well as to offer strategies to increase the graduation rate in America's schools. The center offers free access to monthly webcasts dealing with the dropout crisis and publishes the *Journal of At-Risk Issues*.

National Education Association (NEA)

1201 Sixteenth St. NW
Washington, DC 20036-3290
phone: (202) 833-4000 • fax: (202) 822-7974
website: www.nea.org

The NEA is committed to advancing the cause of public education at every level from preschool to university graduate programs. The NEA has compiled a 12-Point Action Plan for reducing the dropout rate—including making a high school diploma compulsory for everyone under age twenty-one.

US Department of Education

400 Maryland Ave. SW
Washington, DC 20202
phone: (800) 872-5326
website: www.ed.gov

The US Department of Education works to promote student achievement and preparation for global competitiveness by fostering educational excellence. The department establishes policies for the nation's schools and administers and coordinates most federal education assistance.

US Department of Labor

Frances Perkins Bldg.
200 Constitution Ave. NW
Washington, DC 20210
phone: (866) 487-2365 • fax: (202) 563-2776
website: www.doleta.gov

The US Department of Labor is charged with preparing the American workforce for new and better jobs and making sure that workers have adequate conditions in which to do those jobs. The department is also interested in helping youth prepare for the workforce—a key reason why it supports the YouthBuild program.

For Further Research

Books
Lisa Delpit, *Multiplication Is for White People: Raising Expectations for Other People's Children*. New York: New Press, 2012.

Carrie Goldman, *Bullied: What Every Parent, Teacher, and Kid Needs to Know About Ending the Cycle of Fear*. New York: HarperOne, 2012.

Gloria Ladson-Billings, *The Dreamkeepers: Successful Teachers of African-American Children*. San Francisco: Wiley, 2009.

Nelson Reidar, *Education Malpractice: A Year in a Dropout Factory*. Bloomington, IN: AuthorHouse, 2011.

Russell W. Rumberger, *Dropping Out: Why Students Drop Out of High School and What Can Be Done About It*. Cambridge, MA: Harvard University Press, 2011.

James Diego Vigil, *Streetsmart Schoolsmart: Urban Poverty and the Education of Adolescent Boys*. New York: Teachers College, Columbia University, 2012.

Periodicals
Cheryl Almeida, Robert Balanz, and Adria Steinberg, "Dropout Factories: New Strategies States Can Use," *Education Week*, December 16, 2009.

Christian Science Monitor, "How to Reduce Student Dropout Rates: Link Volunteering to Studies," February 10, 2012.

Erik Eckholm, "Discipline of Military Directs Dropouts," *New York Times*, March 8, 2009.

Benjamin Herold, "Job Prospects Bleak for Dropouts in Philadelphia," *Education Week*, February 10, 2012.

Nakia Hill, "A GED Safety Net for High School Students," *Christian Science Monitor*, April 26, 2012.

Joel Hood and Noreen S. Ahmed-Ullah, "Educators Say Funding Key to Reducing Dropouts," *Chicago Tribune*, February 1, 2012.

Lesli A. Maxwell, "Six States Join NGA Dropout-Prevention Initiative," *Education Week*, January 5, 2010.

Henry M. Levin and Cecilia E. Rouse, "The True Cost of High School Dropouts," *New York Times*, January 25, 2012.

Tamar Lewin, "Obama Wades into Issue of Raising Dropout Age," *New York Times*, January 25, 2015.

New York Daily News, "1 in 4 Teens Are Dropping Out of High School," March 19, 2012.

Pedro A. Noguera, "Saving Black and Latino Boys: What Schools Can Do to Make a Difference," *Phi Delta Kappan*, February 2012.

James C. Wilson, "San Diego's High School Population Crisis," *Techniques*, April 2012.

Internet Sources

Kelly Chen, "Behind the Numbers: Why Dropouts Have It Worse than Ever Before," *American Graduate*, December 16, 2011. www.pbs.org/newshour/rundown/2011/12/behind-the-numbers-why-dropouts-have-it-worse-than-ever-before.html.

John Donovan, "Building Apps to Hack the High School Dropout Rate," ATT Innovation Space, June 18, 2012. www.attinnovationspace.com/innovation/story/a7782774.

Rita Giordano, "A New Camden County Program Will Give High School Dropouts a Second Chance," Philly.com, July 25, 2012. http://articles.philly.com/2012-07-25/news/32828877_1_national-program-community-academic-programs-program-director.

PBS Newshour, "In South Texas, Luring Dropouts Back by Sending Them to College," July 4, 2012. www.pbs.org/newshour/bb/american-graduate/july-dec12/amgrad_07-04.html.

Bob Wise and Bob Fulmer, "How Cutting Teen Dropout Rates Could Stimulate the Economy," *Huffington Post*, June 14, 2010. www.huffingtonpost.com/bob-wise/how-cutting-teen-dropout_b_611699.html.

Source Notes

Overview

1. Glenn, personal interview with the author, Saint Paul, MN, August 1, 2012.
2. Quoted in Sherman Dorn, *Creating the Dropout: An Institutional and Social History of School Failure*. Westport, CT: Praeger, 1996, p. 79.
3. Barack Obama, "Remarks by the President at the America's Promise Alliance Education Event," March 1, 2010. www.whitehouse.gov.
4. Quoted in Tavis Smiley, *Too Important to Fail: Investigating the Alarming Dropout Rate of African American Males* (DVD), PBS, 2011.
5. Quoted in Scott O'Connell, "Dropout Rates Fall Across the State," *MetroWest Daily News* (Framingham, MA), February 11, 2012. www.metrowestdaily news.com.
6. Telephone interview with the author, July 18, 2012.
7. Quoted in *New York Daily News*, "1 in 4 Teens Are Dropping Out of High School," March 19, 2012. http://articl es.nydailynews.com.
8. Quoted in Jason Koebler, "How to Identify a High School Dropout Factory," *Education* (blog), *U.S. News & World Report*, November 30, 2011. www.usnews.com.
9. Quoted in *Frontline*, "Middle School Moment," PBS, July 17, 2012. www.pbs.org.
10. Quoted in Karen Farkas, "Programs Geared to Helping High School Dropouts, Other Students Succeed in College," *Metro* (blog), Cleveland.com, January 29, 2012. http://blog.cleveland.com.

Does the United States Have a Dropout Problem?

11. Marco, personal interview with the author, Arden Hills, MN, July 3, 2012.
12. Claudio Sanchez, "Why Dropout Data Can Be So Unreliable," National Public Radio, July 28, 2011. www.npr.org.
13. Quoted in Azam Ahmed, "In Chicago High School: Class Attendance or Numbers Game?," *Chicago Tribune*, June 14, 2009. http://articles.chicago tribune.com.
14. Harry Welch, personal interview with the author, Minneapolis, MN, July 6, 2012.
15. Raymond Smith, telephone interview with the author, July 8, 2012.
16. Quoted in Sam Dillon, "Study Finds High Rate of Imprisonment Among Dropouts," *New York Times*, October 8, 2009. www.nytimes.com.
17. Obama, "Remarks by the President at the America's Promise Alliance Education Event," March 1, 2010. www.whitehouse.gov.

Why Do Teens Drop Out of School?

18. Arlyss Harkness, personal interview with the author, Minneapolis, MN, August 2, 2012.
19. Harkness, interview.
20. Personal interview with the author, Minneapolis, MN, August 20, 2012.
21. Quoted in Emily Richmond, "Dropping Out to Go to Work," *Las Vegas (NV) Sun*, May 15, 2008. www.lasveg assun.com.
22. Quoted in Richmond, "Dropping Out to Go to Work."
23. Quoted in Richmond, "Dropping Out to Go to Work."
24. Quoted in R.W. Dellinger, "Connection Between School Dropouts, Gangs, Motivates L.A. Youths to Lobby in State Capitol," Catholic Online, March 18, 2008. www.catholic.org.
25. Russell W. Rumberger, *Dropping Out:*

Why Students Drop Out of High School and What Can Be Done About It. Cambridge, MA: Harvard University Press, 2011, p. 176.

26. Quoted in Claudio Sanchez, "From Drug Dealing to Diploma: A Teen's Struggle," National Public Radio, July 25, 2011. www.npr.org.

27. Monica, personal interview with the author, Bloomington, MN, August 23, 2012.

28. Quoted in *Not in Our Town* (blog), "Bullying and Dropping Out: Is There a Connection?," March 29, 2012. www.niot.org/blog.

29. Telephone interview with the author, July 23, 2012.

30. Quoted in *The Forum* (blog), Learning Matters, "Discuss: How Do We Best Prevent Dropouts?," April 21, 2009. http://learningmatters.tv.

Can the Dropout Rate Be Reduced?

31. Gabe, personal interview with the author, South Saint Paul, MN, August 29, 2012.

32. Robert Balfanz, "How 'Early Warning Systems' Are Keeping Kids in School," *Washington Post*, April 10, 2012. www.washingtonpost.com.

33. Balfanz, "How 'Early Warning Systems' Are Keeping Kids in School."

34. Quoted in Mary Ann Zehr, "Coaching for Success," *Education Week*, June 10, 2010, p. 5.

35. Quoted in Zehr, "Coaching For Success," p. 6.

36. Nel Noddings, "Differentiate, Don't Standardize," *Education Week*, January 7, 2010. www.edweek.org.

37. Barack Obama, "Remarks by the President in State of the Union Address" (transcript), White House, January 24, 2012. www.whitehouse.gov.

38. William Berkson, "Let's Get Real About the Dropout Crisis," *Education Week*, June 11, 2009. www.edweek.org.

39. Quoted in Shannon McFarland, "Obama Proposal to Raise Dropout Age Falls Flat," MPR News, June 16, 2012. http://minnesota.publicradio.org.

What Can Be Done to Help Dropouts?

40. Quoted in Linda Lutton, "Luring Chicago Dropouts Back to School, One Doorstep at a Time," WBEZ91.5, August 25, 2011. www.wbez.org.

41. Mary Jorgens, personal interview with the author, September 2, 2012.

42. Quoted in Claudio Sanchez, "In Today's Economy, How Far Can a GED Take You?," *NPR Weekend Edition*, February 18, 2012. www.npr.org.

43. Quoted in Sanchez, "In Today's Economy, How Far Can a GED Take You?"

44. Sandra Ransel, "Helping Dropouts Drop Back In," *Educational Leadership*, February 2010. www.ascd.org.

45. Quoted in Brandon Hubbard, "Youth-Build Petoskey Seeks to Put High School Dropouts Back to Work," *Petoskey (MI) News*, January 6, 2012, http://articles.petoskeynews.com.

46. Quoted in Camille Debreczeny, "Youth-Build Helps High School Dropouts Get a Fresh Start," *San Jose Mercury News*, July 7, 2012. www.mercurynews.com.

47. Quoted in Erik Eckholm, "Discipline of Military Redirects Dropouts," *New York Times*, March 8, 2009. www.nytimes.com.

48. Quoted in *NPR Weekend Edition*, "Former Dropouts Push Others to Reach Finish Line," June 24, 2012. www.npr.org.

49. Quoted in *NPR Weekend Edition*, "Former Dropouts Push Others to Reach Finish Line."

List of Illustrations

Index

Picture Credits

About the Author

Gail B. Stewart is the author of more than two hundred fifty books for teens and young adults. She lives with her husband in Minneapolis and is the mother of three grown sons.